The Parrot Breeder's Answer Book

Gayle A. Soucek

BARRON'S

About the Author

Gayle Soucek has been breeding and training parrots for over 15 years. She has been recognized as a Certified Avian Specialist (C.A.S.) by the Pet Industry Joint Advisory Council (PIJAC), and she is currently serving a second term as president of the Midwest Avian Research Expo federation (MARE). She is past president of the Midwest Congress of Bird Clubs and the Northern Illinois Parrot Society and is a current member of The Society of Parrot Breeders and Exhibitors, the American Federation of Aviculture, and the African Parrot Society.

Gayle has written several books and articles, which have appeared in numerous magazines. She and her husband live in the Chicago area and currently share their home with macaws, cockatoos, Amazons, Quakers, several types of African parrots, parrotlets, a few other assorted parrot species, and one very tolerant dog. Her special areas of interest are avian health, nutrition, and captive breeding.

Photo Credits

Sandy Andrews: page 7 (left); Cara Parrots: page 108; Bonnie Doane: pages 47, 138; Scott McDonald, D.V.M.: pages 7 (right), 12, 13, 20, 22, 26, 42, 57, 64, 69, 71 (top, bottom), 72, 75, 76, 77, 80, 82, 85, 87, 102, 114, 117, 122, 135, 137; Katy McElroy: pages 16, 28, 33, 35, 58, 91, 133; Peter J. Rimsa: pages 8, 9, 17, 23, 34, 40, 45, 50, 52, 62, 70, 81, 86, 93, 99, 116, 121, 123 (top, bottom), 125 (top, bottom), 128; Jeannine Southcomb: page 2; Lori Stana: pages 30, 31, 32, 39; Patrick Strangaritch: pages 5, 15, 21.

Cover Photos

Front: Joan Balzarini; Inside Front: B. Everett Webb; Inside Back: Joan Balzarini; Back: Joan Balzarini.

All inquiries should be addressed to:
Barron's Educational Series, Inc.
250 Wireless Boulevard
Hauppauge, New York 11788
http://www.barronseduc.com

International Standard Book No. 0-7641-1695-9

Library of Congress Catalog Card No. 2001035655

Library of Congress Cataloging-in-Publication Data
Soucek, Gayle.
     The parrot breeder's answer book / Gayle Soucek.
         p. cm.
     Includes bibliographical references (p.   ).
     ISBN 0-7641-1695-9 (alk. paper)
         1. Parrots. 2. Parrots—Breeding. I. Title.

SF473.P3 S67   2001
636.6′8652—dc21   2001035655

Printed in Hong Kong

9 8 7 6 5 4 3 2 1

Important Note

The information contained in this book is not intended as a substitute for proper veterinary care. The science of avian medicine is advancing rapidly, and new developments and discoveries continue to improve the health and longevity of captive birds. People who keep parrots are stewards of often valuable and rare wild animals, many of which are endangered or threatened with extinction. As a responsible parrot owner, you should not take this privilege lightly. Always provide proper care and veterinary attention as needed. Use discretion when selling baby parrots to inexperienced owners so that the chicks are placed into suitable homes. It is part of your responsibility to educate and inform new owners on parrot care and behavior to help ensure a long, healthy, and happy existence for the new life you've helped create.

Contents

Preface

When I first began breeding parrots many years ago, my goal was to become an expert. In my innocence, I believed that all the answers were out there in black and white. If I studied long enough and hard enough, I would soon know everything that could be known about parrot aviculture.

Boy, was I wrong! After many humbling years of working with these magnificent birds, the one lesson I've learned is that we should never get so arrogant in our beliefs that we are blinded to fresh information or new ways of doing things. Aviculture is a science. Like any science, it is a constantly evolving and often rapidly changing discipline. As the legendary UCLA basketball coach John Wooden once said, "It's what you learn after you know it all that counts."

In the process of researching this book, I was once again reminded of how much there is to know and how much more we will likely discover in the course of time. What I have shared with you in the following chapters is a combination of research, personal experience, and a little dab of common sense. Techniques that have worked well for me might not work for you, but only experience will teach you that. What I've presented as fact is taken from current published research. In cases where I'm stating personal opinion, I've tried to identify it as such.

I could not have completed this project without the generous help of many special friends. I owe a special thanks to Scott McDonald, D.V.M., and Bonnie Munro Doane for their encouragement, support, friendship, and advice. Jeannine Southcomb, Lori Stana, Katy McElroy, Sandy Andrews, Patrick Strangaritch, and Barb Carapezza all shared photographs and personal experiences and were there for me when I needed them. I'd also like to thank my dear family for believing in me, especially Shar, Marge, Donna, Tammy, and Cindi.

Of course, no book would exist if it weren't for the great folks at Barron's, who have been a joy to work with. I owe them my deepest gratitude. I'd especially like to thank my wonderful husband, Peter, for his patience, support, and assistance in the evolution of this project. And finally, thanks to Piper, Mikey, and Gizmo, who helped initiate me into their world.

Gayle Soucek

Chapter One

Why Breed Parrots? (The Good News)

The practice of keeping parrots for pets has been traced back to at least the early Romans. However, only during the last century or so has aviculture, the intentional breeding of nondomestic birds, grown into a recognized specialty. In earlier times, parrots were rare pets, brought back from exotic travels to faraway places. They often signified a certain amount of wealth and social standing. In the late nineteenth century, that all began to change. Mass trapping and unrestricted importation brought parrots into the mainstream, making them a reasonably common and affordable pet. As refinements in transportation grew, so did the numbers and species of parrots and other exotic fauna making their way across the world's oceans for new homes throughout Europe and the United States.

Where Did All the Parrots Go?

Indeed, by the 1980s, over 500,000 parrots were legally traded each year, according to figures compiled by TRAFFIC International and the World Wildlife Fund. Actual numbers are difficult to determine. These estimates do not include local trade, birds that died before export, or those that were illegally traded. Therefore, the true number of birds removed from the wild during those years is certainly much higher, perhaps closer to one million per year. These figures are for parrots only. Various sources quoted by TRAFFIC International estimate that the total number of live birds traded worldwide during the 1970s ranged from seven to ten million per year!

By the late 1970s, it was becoming increasingly apparent that this widespread exploitation of wild populations could not continue without causing irreparable damage. A few exporting countries began initiating trade controls. Another decade passed, however, before global awareness of the problem surfaced. By 1990, nearly one-third of the world's known parrot species were considered endangered and under threat of extinction. Most of the remaining two-thirds had rapidly declining populations and shrinking

Parrots have been kept as pets since ancient times. Companion birds must now be bred in captivity because federal laws prohibit importation of parrots for the pet trade.

habitats. Under growing international pressure, the United States passed the Wild Bird Conservation Act of 1992, effectively banning the importation of parrots and many other birds into this country. (The exceptions, mostly for zoos and scientific programs, are too few to discuss here.) Even though many other countries followed suit with trade restrictions of their own, it might be a case of "too little, too late." Noted aviculturist and author Rosemary Low estimates that some species of Indonesian cockatoos, for example, exist in much greater numbers in captivity than in the wild. For species like this, captive breeding might be the only hope for preventing extinction.

The Role of Aviculture

What does all this mean to someone who wants to breed parrots? For starters, it means that you should not take this responsibility lightly. Captive breeding stock is precious and might not be replaceable once it has gone. Even if you want to breed only a few very common species, your level of professionalism and expertise will most likely dictate your level of success. With this in mind, you should begin your journey by taking a hard look at where you want to go.

All too often, people start breeding parrots almost by accident. They pick up a mate for their hormonal pet, hear about a hot deal on a pair of birds at a local club, or make an impulse purchase off the Internet. Soon, they find themselves with a random collection of species, some of which might inhibit the breeding activity of others. Seeing ads offering birds for sale because the breeder is "refocusing the collection" is common. What this usually means is that these individuals are trying to undo the mistakes they made through lack of initial planning. I can speak about this with some authority since I made all the same mistakes (and then some) when I was starting out.

Defining Your Goals

To avoid these pitfalls, begin by defining your goals and abilities. For example, it's a safe bet that breeding the large macaws isn't a viable option if you're currently living in a studio apartment. However, a pair of lovebirds might happily settle into your limited space.

It has been said that you can catch a terrible, often incurable disease from parrots—"acquisitionitis." The symptoms include buying more birds than you have room for, or can properly care for, and going into debt to purchase more birds even while you are cutting corners to afford the ones you already have. The best preventative medicine for this syndrome is careful planning, self-honesty, and willpower. With this in mind, the time has come to make some decisions.

Important Considerations

Before you decide to breed any bird, ask yourself the following questions:
• How much space can I devote to the birds?
• What species would I most enjoy working with?
• Which of these species can be comfortably housed in my available space?
• Do I have extra space available for quarantine and nursery functions?
• What noise level can I live with? Is this consistent with the species I've chosen?
• How much money can I afford to invest in breeding stock, caging, food, nursery supplies, and veterinary bills?
• How much time can I commit to caring for my birds and their offspring?
• What are my expectations?
• Why am I doing this?

How honestly you answer these questions will have a great impact on your success. If you don't know where you want to end up, then both you and your birds will probably suffer. Far too many birds have been stuffed into too-small cages in garages, spare bedrooms, and even bathrooms only because their owners couldn't resist just one more bargain even though the house was already bursting at the seams.

Breeding: A Hobby or a Profession?

A common distinction is made in the bird business between hobby breeding and professional aviculture. Although most people consider it a difference of size and scope, I would argue that it's more a difference of skill and responsibility. Some small breeders keep meticulous records and participate in studbooks (a record-keeping collective designed to help maintain genetic diversity of rare species). Alternatively, a few large "professional" collections were little more than birdie mills. Whether you have two birds or 2,000 birds, you can achieve professionalism. For the point of this question, I'd rather substitute the term *commercial aviculture* to consider the distinction of size and time commitment. These distinctions are admittedly somewhat arbitrary but are intended to give you a rough idea of the range of possibilities.

A hobby breeder most likely has a relatively small number of birds and cares for them part-time in addition to another job or avocation. The money earned from the birds, although it might be significant, is not a primary source of income. Hobby breeders range from families who have two pairs of producing budgies in their spare bedroom to people who have 200 or more birds in backyard flights and devote a huge chunk of time every day to providing care.

A commercial aviculturist most likely owns or is employed by a large breeding facility with hundreds or even thousands of birds and multiple employees. These facilities are (or should be) income producing and are most likely the primary source of income for the aviculturist. These large breeding farms tend to be most common in Sunbelt states like Texas, Florida, and California but sometimes can be found even in harsh, northern climates.

As you can see, parrot breeding can be done on a very small scale or a very large one. Your available resources, including money, time, and space, will largely help determine the maximum size of your breeding program. Once you're clear about size, the next point to consider is your ultimate focus, or why you're breeding parrots in the first place.

Breeding for Conservation

Once you fall in love with parrots, developing an idealistic nature and deciding you want to devote your energies to conserving rare species is easy. Countless beginners have asked me over the years how to breed their birds for eventual re-release into the wild. Unfortunately, given the current level of knowledge, that goal might be out of reach for individual aviculturists. Conservation is an extremely complicated and multifaceted problem. Even the

A hobby breeder might have just a few pairs of birds set up in a spare bedroom or den.

experts cannot agree on the best way to overcome all the challenges.

For an example, look at the plight of the Goffin's cockatoo. These delightful, small cockatoos have wonderful pet potential. They exist in the wild only on the Tanimbar Islands, a small Indonesian island group with an area of about 2,172 square miles (5,604 m^2), just slightly larger than the state of Delaware.

During the period from 1983 to 1989, more than 73,500 of these little charmers were imported into the United States. At about the same time, Japanese logging companies acquired timber rights for Tanimbar and began clear-cutting the forests. Cockatoos, like most parrots, are cavity nesters that lay their eggs in hollowed-out trees. Without trees, no habitat exists to support the birds. Their nest sites, food sources, and protection from predators are all gone. At this point in time, Goffin's are common in captivity but extremely endangered in the wild.

As an aviculturist, how would you help conserve the Goffin's? To begin with, releasing tame birds into the wild is a death sentence. They have no skills for hunting, avoiding predators, or finding nest sites. An early-release program of thick-billed parrots in Arizona turned into a disaster when hawks rapidly killed off most of the birds. Since then, the

Getting Involved

The private aviculturist can aid in conservation efforts in a number of ways.

• Begin by learning all you can about the species you wish to breed.

• Keep careful and detailed records, and never inbreed your stock.

• If your birds are a threatened species, find out if a studbook is being kept and participate. (Information about studbooks is usually available from the World Parrot Trust or the American Federation of Aviculture—see "Resource Guide").

• If possible, allow the parent birds to rear some young completely through weaning. Parent-raised chicks learn proper parrot behaviors and often grow up to be excellent parents themselves.

• Trade or sell these chicks to others who are dedicated to working with that species.

By helping to maintain a healthy, diverse, and productive gene pool, at the very least these parrots can be kept strong in captivity. This might someday be an invaluable aid in preserving endangered parrots in the wild, especially as conservationists and field researchers gain more knowledge about reintroduction strategies.

Arizona program and others like it have spent much time, money, and research on teaching potential release birds the skills they need to survive. In spite of the best efforts of researchers in the field, re-release programs have had limited success.

Even if suitable release birds were available, they would be of little value if the range habitat has been destroyed. In the example of the Tanimbars, so much of the land has been cleared of forest that it simply could not support the number of cockatoos once living there, even if the birds could magically be returned. Unless Indonesian authorities undertake a program of land reforestation, the future of Goffin's cockatoos is bleak.

Breeding for the Pet Trade

Even if you work with common species and have no interest in conservation, most of the suggestions in the box at left apply to you. With parrots at peak popularity, the demand for tame, hand-raised pets is extremely high. If your goal is to produce healthy, well-socialized baby parrots for the pet trade, then careful pairing, excellent record keeping, and good husbandry make economic sense in addition to being the ethical course. Unfortunately, some common pet birds have been carelessly inbred in the past, and genetic weaknesses are beginning to surface.

Mutations

These weaknesses appear most often in heavily inbred birds.

A hybrid harlequin macaw (blue and gold macaw x green-winged macaw).

Whenever possible, allow the parents to rear some chicks to maturity to ensure future breeding stock.

Mutations are genetic faults that occur randomly in nature. In birds, these faults most commonly show up as changes in feather color due to missing or altered pigmentation. The cockatiel is a perfect example. Normal cockatiels are mostly gray birds and are usually quite hardy. Although color mutations appear occasionally in the wild, these birds do not usually survive since they stand out from their flock and make a perfect target for predators. Even when they do survive, they're unlikely to find a similar mate. Therefore, they tend either to not breed or to breed with a normal-colored mate, thus not perpetuating the mutation.

In captivity, however, that all changed. Over the years, color mutations such as pure white (albino), solid yellow (lutino), and variegated colors (pied) appeared. Since these birds were unusual and often quite pretty, breeders began to inbreed them intentionally to produce established bloodlines that would pass on these genetic traits. At this point, captive-bred cockatiels are available in over a dozen different color mutations, and normal gray

The Senegal parrot on the left shows normal green coloration. The bird on the right is a pied mutation, which manifests as abnormally colored patches of feathers (in this case, bright yellow instead of green).

cockatiels are slowly beginning to disappear. Unfortunately, some undesirable traits are also passed along with the color mutations, such as bald spots in feathering, night thrashing (sudden panic attacks after dark), and shortened life spans. New research being done at the University of California in Davis suggests that highly inbred color mutation cockatiels may be suffering from an inherited kidney defect that causes poor kidney function and that will progress to gout and kidney failure when the birds are fed a high-protein diet.

Responsible cockatiel breeders are working hard to eliminate these negative traits. However, careless or inept people are still out there paying little or no attention to strengthening the bloodlines of the birds they keep. In the long run, these people end up hurting themselves economically in addition to the damage they cause to the birds. Genetically weak birds produce less, suffer more illnesses, and might display personality defects that make them undesirable as pets or breeding stock. The worst fear is that careless breeding will eventually introduce a lethal gene, which is a genetic flaw that prevents hatching or kills the bird at an early age. Lethal genes have already shown up in the poultry industry. The reports of kidney disease in cockatiels might very well be the tip of that iceberg.

Hybrids

A different sort of problem arises when people breed hybrids. Hybrids are the offspring of parents of different species, subspecies, or races. In dogs, they are called mixed breeds or mongrels. Because the parrot family is so diverse, crossbreeding is not possible except within a genus. (A few exceptions do occur, mostly between closely related genera.) For example, an Amazon could not reproduce with an African grey even though they are of similar size, but two different species of Amazon could crossbreed. Hybridization seems to occur most commonly in the large macaws, which are mostly members of the genus *Ara,* although plenty of hybrid conures (*Aratinga*), Amazons (*Amazona*), cockatoos (*Cacatua*), and others occur.

The rationale for breeding hybrids is that they are beautiful and make unusual pets. If parrot species were as common and easily available as purebred dogs, I wouldn't have a problem with this argument. Unfortunately, as I mentioned earlier, most parrots are endangered, some critically. The scarlet macaw, for example, is often paired with a blue and gold macaw to produce a hybrid known as the catalina. Catalina macaws are beautiful, but so are scarlets, and scarlets are listed by the Convention on International Trade in Endangered Species (CITES) as "threatened with extinction." To add to the destruction of this critically scarce gene pool intentionally by crossbreeding it is short-sighted, to say the least. The existing hybrids deserve all the love and respect that one would give to any parrot, but the breeding of more of them must be stopped. Parrot breeders do not deal with domestic animals from common gene pools. These are wild animals, many of which are facing extinction in their range countries. People should not view themselves as owners but as stewards and accept the responsibilities that come with that honor.

Once you've made the commitment to be a responsible bird keeper, your reputation will grow and people will seek you out to purchase your chicks. Your birds will be healthier and more productive. All in all, you'll find that the effort you put in, and the love and dedication you bring to the process, will reward you in many ways—some obvious and some quite unexpected.

A hybrid Sunday conure (sun conure x Jenday conure).

Breeding Ease and Chick Prices for Select Parrots

Species	Availability of Breeding Pairs	Ease of Breeding	Average Sell Price of Hand-Raised Chicks
Africans			
Greys	Plentiful	Prolific	$600–$900
Poicephalus	Plentiful	Prolific	$300–$500
Macaws			
Minis	Plentiful	Prolific	$500–$900
Large	Plentiful	Prolific	$700–$1,500
Amazons	Plentiful	Difficult	$500–$1,000
Cockatiels	Plentiful	Prolific	$40–$100
Cockatoos	Moderate	Moderate	$600–$1,500
Conures	Plentiful	Moderate	$100–$400
Eclectus	Plentiful	Moderate	$600–$900
Lories	Moderate	Moderate	$200–$600
Lovebirds	Plentiful	Prolific	$40–$100
Parrotlets	Plentiful	Prolific	$100–$200 (Mutations higher)
Pionus	Moderate	Prolific	$200–$500
Quaker	Plentiful	Prolific	$100–$200

This information pertains to common species of the above genera. Individual species might vary considerably. Prices are based on a February 2001 survey of breeder pricing and may not reflect regional variations.

Chapter Two

Why You Should Not Breed Parrots (The Bad News)

If a strong love of parrots doesn't form the basis for at least part of your motivation for wanting to breed them, then you will most likely be unsuccessful. Easier ways exist to earn a buck. Parrot breeding doesn't come with any guarantees. It's hard work. If you do not enjoy the process, the financial payoffs (if and when they come) probably won't be enough to make it worth your time. Don't get me wrong; it is possible to make money breeding birds. It's just a poor reason to do so.

Do It for Love, Not Money

The following is a brief look at the economics of aviculture. As an example, the cost versus income potential for a pair of Congo African grey parrots will be described. Greys are extremely intelligent birds with a talent for talking, and they usually make delightful pets. Because of this, they're in high demand in the pet trade. In the Chicago area, a typical pair of breeding greys costs about $1,500. A cage big enough to house them comfortably will run anywhere from about $150 for a simple homemade wire enclosure to more than $900 for a nice, wrought-iron model. If you live in a warm climate and plan to build outdoor flights, you'll spend a great deal more. Budget a very conservative $400. A nest box will cost between $50 and $100. For perches, toys, additional feeding dishes, and other paraphernalia, add another $100. The first veterinary visit to ensure that the birds are healthy will most likely run at least $100 per bird, possibly much more, depending on what diagnostics the veterinarian deems necessary. You have already spent more than $2,300 and are just starting!

Once you get the birds home, you'll have to feed them. Greys are hearty and enthusiastic eaters. I estimate that the cost of food, treats, supplements, cleaning supplies, and a *very* minimal dollar value of my time spent servicing the birds averages about $3 per pair per day, or nearly $1,100 per year. This means that, in the first year, the birds would have to produce $3,400 in income for you just to break even. Baby greys sell for about $800, so you would need five chicks the first year to pay off your investment in the adult birds alone. This does not count the cost of baby gear like incubators, brooders, baby food, and all the rest. Although a really prolific pair of greys might produce four to six chicks a year, many will produce far less, and it's not uncommon for a pair to take a year's break occasionally. Don't let anyone tell you that it's likely they'll produce more. Even if

you could somehow stimulate higher production, it would only harm the birds. Overbreeding takes a serious toll on health, especially for the female bird, whose body is drained of calcium and other nutrients during egg production. Responsible parrot breeders usually shut down (discourage breeding in) pairs that are in egg-laying overdrive.

A quick glance at the numbers above might seem discouraging, but that's not my intention here. As you (and your birds) become more experienced, you'll find ways to maximize profits without compromising quality of care. You'll also gain economies of scale if you have more than one breeding pair. Certain species are more prolific, and a proper mix of species can keep cash flow going

Baby African greys command a high price on the pet market, but raising them isn't cheap or easy.

through different breeding seasons. If you read and follow the advice in this book, I hope I can help you avoid some of the costly mistakes I made when I was starting out. So, although making a profit by parrot breeding is certainly possible, it should never be your primary motivation.

The Noise, the Mess, the Bills . . . Oh My!

Besides the obvious financial commitment necessary to keep birds, you must be willing to make an investment in time and sanity. Parrots are by nature noisy, messy critters. One of their most endearing traits is the exuberance with which they live their lives. Unfortunately, this same exuberance makes them greet dawn and dusk with ear-splitting screams of birdie joy, play-fully fling food against the ceiling to see what sticks, and tear up or dis-assemble anything in their path, just because they can.

Even remarkably sedate parrots will molt feathers, spill food, and become vocal at certain times. I keep a colorful stuffed toy parrot on the desk in my office. When poten-tial buyers come to see my chicks and tell me they want a bird that won't ever bite, get noisy, or make a mess, I hand them the stuffed bird and inform them that this is the only parrot that's going to satisfy their requirements.

Parrots can be noisy and destructive.

If you're the type of person who requires peace and quiet and you keep your home looking like a photo shoot for a magazine, you might want to reconsider the idea of breeding parrots. Even if you own enough land to keep the adult birds housed outdoors or in a separate building, rest assured that hand-feeding chicks, unsold adolescents, and the odd spare adult bird will all infiltrate your living space. If this prospect doesn't fill you with joy, then you're moving into dangerous territory.

Parrots Are . . .

- Messy
- Noisy
- Extroverted
- Intelligent
- Funny
- Exhausting
- Rascally
- High-maintenance

Spousal Support (or Lack Thereof . . .)

Even if you find yourself unfazed by the above cautions, you'll want to think long and hard about the effect on your family. If you live alone and have the time to devote to the birds, the decision is, of course, completely yours. If you have a spouse, children, or any significant others sharing your home, then you need to come to an understanding with housemates about the realities of living with parrots. If they're as excited about the prospect as you are, then you have the makings for a great family endeavor. If they don't share your passion, however, you have the makings for a disaster. They might resent the disruption, time, and expense. You will constantly be torn between the demands of both sides.

In my case, my husband and I got married well after I had become heavily involved in breeding large parrots, so he had some idea what he was getting into, but it was still quite an adjustment for him. Although he really loves the birds, he'd honestly be happier as a pet owner with just one or two special birds in the house. The noise and upkeep drive him a little crazy, but he good-naturedly tolerates it, at least most of the time. Since birds are my passion, not his, that means that most of the work falls onto my shoulders, which is only fair. He's great about helping out when I need

it, though, so I consider myself lucky. Will you be as lucky? Be certain that you and your family are clear about what parrot breeding entails, or you might face unpleasant choices down the road. Now is the time to set guidelines and make compromises, not after you've invested time, money, and emotion into the birds.

You Will Never Leave Home Again

Even if your family is supportive and you are convinced that the pitfalls mentioned are mere trifles standing between you and your dream, you must consider one more thing. What happens if you are not there? My husband and I haven't taken a real vacation in over 10 years. We've managed a few long weekends here and there, depending on the goodwill of friends and family members, but a real getaway has been out of reach. Although I have a relatively modest number of birds (about 70), properly caring for and cleaning them takes about three hours per day. Even though I combine this with a full-time job as well as a busy freelance writing schedule, most of my friends are not similarly inclined. To expect someone to spend three hours a day for a solid week or two caring for my birds while I'm away is more than I could ask of anyone. Sure, I could hire someone, but that gets pricey really quickly. Besides, I have huge, boisterous macaws, nasty Amazons, spoiled cockatoos, and nervous Africans that require a lot more knowledge and experience to handle than the average pet-sitter has to offer. My parrot breeder friends all have their own flocks to contend with, although they have been really gracious about baby-sitting chicks for occasional weekends.

The best answer is to hire and train someone responsible well in advance of a trip. If you do this, make certain you have a backup plan in case your bird-sitter is suddenly unable to fulfill the duties. Have a trusted friend or family member check in every day or so to make sure the birds are getting proper care. Even if you're completely secure about the person's reliability, accidents and illnesses do occur. You do not want to be thousands of miles away from home on an expensive vacation of a lifetime only to find that your caretaker has gone AWOL and your birds are helpless and without food or water.

Of course, leaving town is not the only time you might need help. What happens to your birds if you become sick or disabled? A few years ago, my husband was out of town on an important business trip. As luck would have it, I contracted a really nasty case of food poisoning at the same time. I was so violently ill that I rarely left the bathroom floor. Unfortunately, the birds were unsympathetic and hungry, so I practically crawled to the aviary and feverishly struggled to toss some fresh food and water into the cages between repeated trips to the bathroom. The birds, after taking a look at my appearance, apparently decided that I might indeed drop before I handed out their treats, so they all began to scream loudly in encouragement and to hurry me along. It was not a pleasant experience. If you are planning to be the sole caretaker for your flock, I suggest that you find someone who can pinch-hit for you in emergencies.

Why Parrots Are Different

One of the final points to consider before you decide to breed parrots is the effect it will have on your relationship with the birds. Except in very rare instances, breeder birds

Who will care for your birds when you are not around?

Parrots usually mate for life and shun human interaction once they've bonded to each other.

are not pets. Most parrots are monogamous, and they mate for life. These highly intelligent and sensitive creatures form incredibly strong relationships, or *pair-bonds*. Once a pair of parrots has bonded to each other, they should be left together for the remainder of their lives. They are completely different from dogs, cats, and many other animals, which can be placed together for a very short period of time for the sole purpose of breeding. Nonbonded parrots will usually not produce eggs and might not care for their offspring if they do happen to produce. On the other hand, a bonded pair displays many of the best traits of a good human marriage. The two are loyal and affectionate toward each other, share parenting responsibilities, and in most cases make good parents.

Unfortunately, most pair-bonded parrots also lose their desire for human companionship. People often tell me they'd like to breed their beloved pet parrot "just once." They have the misconception that parrots are like dogs and think that they can put them with another bird for a brief time and get a few babies out of the deal. It just doesn't work that way with parrots. If you decide to breed a pet, you need to understand that it will no longer be a pet. Even the tamest bird will most likely turn nasty toward humans once it bonds with a mate of its own.

You must remember that parrots are wild animals. They will quickly revert to the wild if allowed to follow their natural instincts. Aviculture has the habit of referring to captive-bred parrots as domestic birds. However, true domesticity does not occur after just a few (or even a few dozen) generations. This doesn't mean that you shouldn't turn a bird from a pet into a breeder. Some tame parrots reach sexual maturity and show obvious signs that they'd like to raise a family. For these birds, allowing them to pair with a mate might be the kindest thing you can do for them. You just need to be aware that your relationship with the bird will change drastically. Many well-meaning people have set up a pet bird for breeding and then continually attempt to coax the former pet into affectionate interactions. This is stressful and confusing to the parrot since it is being torn between its previous bond to the owner and its emerging bond to its parrot mate. This becomes a real no-win situation. If its loyalty to the human wins out, it will not bond properly with the other bird and might even begin fighting with the cage mate. If it bonds with its new mate, frequent interference by a human might cause jealousy and stress in the new pairing. If you decide to place your pet into a breeding situation, think of yourself as the bird's divorced spouse. You can certainly maintain a civil, even friendly relationship, but keep your visits brief and do not overstay your welcome.

Are You a Bird Person?

If you still want to breed parrots after reading all these warnings, then congratulations—you are a bird person. You already know in your heart that the rewards will far outweigh the difficulties, and you are willing to pay the price. You will be one of the lucky few that can hold a newborn chick in your hand and marvel at the amazing perfection of nature. You will have the joy of watching that tiny, helpless creature grow into a beautiful exotic bird with an incredible intellect and a sentient nature. You'll be filled with pride when you send that bird off to a new home where it will bring its new owners a lifetime of love and companionship. Even during the times when the dollars-and-cents side of the equation is a little weak, I think you'll agree that the bottom line is priceless.

For a bird person, watching the babies grow to maturity is just one of the rewards of breeding.

Chapter Three

Obtaining Breeding Stock: Reading the Singles Columns

Once you've decided to breed parrots, your first step then becomes finding a pair of birds that are similarly inclined. If you've read and followed the advice in the two previous chapters, then you've already decided what species you want to work with and how many birds you want to acquire. Now your search begins.

Finding the Right Birds

Although grabbing the first bargain you see is tempting, you'll be much better off if you do a little comparative shopping first. Check several different sources for birds, and make a list of possibilities. Now compare prices, health guarantees, references, and any known history for the birds. For example, a pair that has already raised some chicks will likely cost a little more up front but might be a better investment since it's likely they'll be reliable

producers. The cheapest birds you find could end up being the most expensive ones you own if you end up feeding and caring for them for a few years before they begin to nest.

Remember, however, you get no guarantees that any pair will ever produce chicks. Highly prolific birds have suddenly refused to have anything to do with each other when sold to a new owner. Other birds that wouldn't breed for one person hop enthusiastically into the nest box as soon as they're placed into a new home. Predicting with any certainty what will happen is impossible when you set up highly intelligent creatures like parrots in a breeding situation. They all have their own preferences and peculiarities. You might never know what motivates one pair to raise clutch after clutch of beautiful chicks while another perfectly healthy pair sits nearby and refuses even to glance in the direction of their nest box.

For example, I have two pairs of Goffin's cockatoos that I bought about 12 years ago. At the time I purchased them, both pairs were mature and seemed well bonded. For 10 years, neither pair produced. I tried everything short of voodoo spells to induce them to nest, but nothing worked. I kept thinking I ought to sell them to someone else who might have better luck, but I was attached to the birds and kept procrastinating. Then, two years ago, I walked into the aviary one day and found one pair on eggs. Within a week, the second pair had eggs, too. What had changed? Just a few weeks earlier, I had replaced their chewed and dirty nest boxes with new ones of a slightly different style. In the past, I had changed nest box styles more than once in an attempt to stimulate the birds, with no success. Apparently, I had finally discovered a style that pleased them. Now they go to nest twice a year, like clockwork, and have beautiful, healthy chicks. Guessing what will make a good breeding pair is not always possible. However, if you do your homework and choose healthy birds, you'll at least avoid some of the obvious pitfalls.

Where to Buy

Many different sources are available where you can find breeder parrots. Each has some advantages and some disadvantages. However, no matter where you finally decide to purchase, remember the cardinal rule: Let the buyer beware.

Newspaper Classifieds

The advantage with these is that you are usually dealing with a local person, so you can probably spend more time looking at the birds in their current home environment. The disadvantage is that these ads are often limited and tend more toward pet birds rather than breeding stock.

Bird Fairs

These might have a good selection and will allow you to make contact with the local breeders who frequent these events. Unfortunately, the rate of disease transmission is much higher when birds are brought together in such crowded and stressful conditions. Use extreme caution when purchasing here. One sick bird in an exhibition hall can spread disease to all the others.

Avicultural Magazines

Parrot magazines such as *Bird Talk* and *Bird Times* are available on most newsstands and include an extensive breeder classified section. These ads, which are listed by state, tend to be placed by serious hobbyists or commercial breeders. Therefore, the selection is large, and you're bound to find what you're looking for.

The disadvantage is that unless you're lucky enough to find a breeder nearby, you'll most likely be buying sight unseen and incurring shipping costs. If you go this route, ask for references. Don't proceed unless you feel comfortable. If possible, get pictures of the birds and ask

It is not always possible to predict what stimulates a pair of birds to breed.

detailed questions about their condition. I've purchased several birds from out-of-state breeders, and I've always been very pleased. I've heard plenty of horror stories, however, so I know that not everyone has been so lucky.

Internet Sites

In recent years, several sites have popped up on the Web that are devoted to aviculture. Many of these have classified ad listings similar to the magazines. Although the same pros and cons apply as when purchasing from magazines, the chance of fraud is slightly higher on the Internet due to the rapid and interactive environment. One popular site recently added a ratings section for sellers, which allows people to post both positive and negative experi-

ences. Again, I've purchased several birds this way, and I've had good luck. If you go this route, make certain you have a valid name, home address, and home phone number for the seller. Don't hesitate to check references. Never make a deal with someone who is reluctant to supply information.

Pet Stores

Although pet shops deal primarily in hand-raised baby birds, they might be able to put you in touch with local breeders who have spare adults for sale. Veterinary clinics that treat parrots are another possibility. Many have bulletin boards that are a great source for referrals. Even if the bird species you are looking for is not listed, making a few phone calls anyway is not a bad idea. Parrot people tend to network very efficiently with each other and will most likely be glad to pass along the names of friends who work with a particular species.

Deciphering the Jargon

Once you've found a few good sources, you'll need to understand exactly what they're selling. For example, you might see ads that read like this: "ssm CAG, wc, proven," or "dna f M2, dom, never set up." Although this might look like code, once you're familiar with the lingo of aviculture, it's all perfectly clear.

Determining Gender

In both of the sample ads, the first part refers to the sex of the bird and tells how it was determined. In the first ad, "ssm" stands for surgically sexed male. That means that a veterinarian has inserted an instrument called an endoscope through a small incision in the bird's side to determine its sex visually. Surgical sexing, although invasive, has some advantages. An experienced veterinarian can roughly gauge the bird's age, peek at some internal organs to check health, and diagnose certain causes of infertility. Once the procedure is completed, the vet injects tattoo ink under the wing to mark the bird. These tattoos are under the right wing for males and under the left wing for females. My male veterinarian said the easiest way to keep this straight is to remember that "men are always right." Since he's such a great veterinarian, I just humor him on this.

In the second ad, "dna f" refers to a DNA-sexed female. In this sexing method, a small drop of blood is taken from the bird (usually by just clipping a toenail) and sent to a lab that analyzes the DNA and determines the sex. The lab then issues a certificate of gender analysis that has the owner's name, bird's name or identification number, and sex. This method is easy and safe. It can even be performed on very young chicks. Unfortunately, unlike surgical sexing, it will not tell you anything about health, level of maturity, or breeding ability. For example, a hen might have a scarred or damaged ovary that renders her completely

Ask for recent pictures if you're thinking about buying sight unseen from a distant seller so you won't suffer any surprises about the bird's condition.

infertile. Surgical sexing should catch the problem, but DNA analysis will not. I tend to use DNA sexing for pets, chicks, or young, healthy birds that I already own. If I lay out good money for mature breeding stock, I like to have my veterinarian take a peek inside to make sure I'm not spending time and money setting up an infertile or old bird.

A few other ways will determine the sex of a parrot, but most are not very reliable. By placing your finger between the bird's pelvic bones, guessing the gender is possible. Male birds have a narrow pelvis, while hens have a much broader pelvis so that they can pass eggs without difficulty. Too many birds have been misidentified this way, however, so it is not recommended.

Other methods include gauging head shape and size, looking at subtle color variations in the feathers, and dangling a crystal pendant over the bird and noting the direction it swings. I'm not putting down any of these methods—some people swear by them—but I suggest you stick with DNA or surgical techniques, which are almost foolproof.

Of course, a few species of parrots are sexually dimorphic, which is a fancy way of saying that the boys are different colors than the girls. The Eclectus are the most striking example of dimorphism, with the males bright green and the females deep red. Even in an obvious case like this, however, surgical sexing may be worthwhile just to guarantee that the bird looks healthy inside.

The Name Game

The next part of the ads refers to the species being sold. Parrot people like to come up with acronyms and nicknames for their favorites. These can sometimes be a puzzle to the uninitiated. "CAG" stands for Congo African grey. Timneh African greys are known as "TAGs." "M2" is a Moluccan cockatoo. Umbrella cockatoos are called "U2s," and so on. Eclectus parrots are often referred to as "ekkies." The Amazon folks tend to use initials, such as "BFA" for blue-fronted Amazon and "DYH" for double yellow-headed Amazons. After reading the ads for a while, you'll get to be a pro at figuring out what the heck they're talking about.

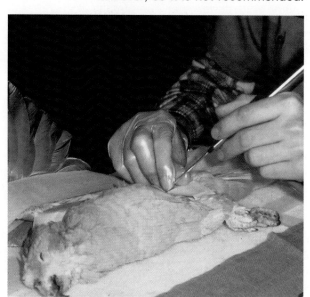

Surgical sexing allows the veterinarian to determine gender and level of maturity and to judge some aspects of overall health.

Import Versus Domestic

The next part of the sample ads tells you where the birds came from. In this example, "wc" stands for wild caught and means that the grey is an imported bird (some ads will simply say "import"). The cockatoo, on the other hand, was born in captivity, which is indicated by the "dom" (domestic) in the ad. In the past, parrot breeders coveted wild-caught stock because these birds had presumably learned the facts of life from their parents and knew what to do when given a nest box and mate. Captive-raised birds were sometimes imprinted on humans and often showed little interest in other parrots. With a little patience, many domestic birds could eventually turn into productive breeders, but the wild caughts were a safer bet. Imported birds were also quite a bit cheaper than hand-raised domestics. Some commercial import facilities even sexed incoming parrots and sold them in pairs for a discounted price, making it easy for anyone who wanted to set up a breeding program.

In 1992, however, new federal laws prohibited the importation of almost all parrots into the United States. Many other countries imposed restrictions of their own. This means that almost any imported bird now in the country is at least 10 years old and probably older (importation peaked in the 1970s and 1980s). Since most parrots can remain reproductively active throughout their teen years and into

In breeder jargon, this is a ssm M2, wc, never set up. (Surgically sexed male Moluccan cockatoo, wild-caught [imported], never set up for breeding.)

their twenties or even thirties for some species, wild-caught birds remain popular, although they are an aging population.

As these imports slowly fade away, the trend has been toward captive-bred, parent-raised breeding pairs. Since at least some mating and chick-rearing behavior in parrots is apparently learned and not instinctual, parent-raised birds might make better parents themselves. This can, however, vary widely between species. I've found, for example, that hand-raised macaws breed readily and usually make excellent parents, but some tame cockatoos and African parrots are slow to accept mates and reluctant to go to nest. Even when they do produce fertile eggs, they sometimes will not incubate or feed the chicks. This does not mean that tame birds cannot be used as breeders. Just be aware that you'll need to be patient and give them plenty of time to adjust. Of course, if you find that a bird isn't adjusting after a few months, seems stressed, and continues to beg for human attention, then the kindest thing might be to return it to pet status. Parrots are individuals. All the how-to books in the world are no substitute for knowing your birds and responding appropriately to their needs.

Breeding Experience

The final portion of the sample ads refers to the breeding experience of the birds. The African grey is listed as "proven," which should mean that he has successfully sired and raised chicks. You'll note that I said "should mean." This term is sometimes misused and applied to pairs that have produced infertile eggs or that lay fertile eggs but refuse to incubate or feed the chicks. Reputable breeders will clarify this by saying something like "proven, won't feed." Also, when a single bird is for sale and listed as proven, this means that it somehow lost its mate. Very few breeders intentionally break up producing pairs. Did the mate die from disease? Perhaps the surviving bird is also ill or carrying the disease. Did the mate die from trauma? Some species (especially cockatoos) are prone to mate aggression, where the male kills the female in a sudden rage. (In a very few noncockatoo species, the hen might be the aggressor.) Unless

you can identify what caused the aggression, mate killers are likely to strike again if paired with a new hen. Ask questions!

The cockatoo ad says "never set up." This means that it is a single bird that has never been placed into a breeding situation. In many cases, these are former pet birds that, for whatever reason, are now being sold as breeding stock. Perhaps they have developed behavioral problems such as biting and screaming. Maybe it is a female that has begun making nests and laying eggs without the benefit of male companionship. It could also be a parent-raised bird that the breeder never got around to placing with a mate. Again, ask questions so that you fully understand the bird's history.

Two other terms you might see are "bonded" and "egg laying." Bonded means that the birds have accepted each other as mates. A bonded pair will perch next to each other, preen each other, and share food. Other than occasional minor spats, they show no signs of fear or aggression toward each other. Although this is a good first step, ask how long the pair has been together. Some parrots will form strong platonic bonds that never result in chicks. If they are sexually mature and have been together for more than a year or so without any sign of breeding behavior, they might just be really good friends. Of course, some birds can take several years to settle in and reproduce (like my cockatoos). However, be aware that bonded does not necessarily lead to proven.

Egg laying is a term that makes me nervous. If applied to a single female, then it might be a good thing. Placing her with a suitable mate could result in chicks in no time at all. If applied to a pair, however, it might signify a problem. Egg laying usually means that the birds have produced clear (infertile) eggs or that they have laid eggs and promptly destroyed, eaten, or deserted them. Here is where you need to ask careful questions. If the birds laid just one or two clear clutches, they seem bonded, and they attempt to incubate the eggs, then this might not indicate a problem, especially if they are young and inexperienced. If it has happened more than a few times or if they are damaging the eggs, then you should steer clear. Egg eating is a significant behavioral problem that is difficult (if not impossible) to correct. Sometimes, you can split the birds up and pair them with new mates, but the behavior usually persists.

If you're considering a pair with a questionable history, arrange to have an experienced avian veterinarian check them out thoroughly *before* you make the deal. On more than one occasion, prospective sellers have met me at my veterinarian's office with the birds. They agree that if I buy the pair, I pay for the exam. If the birds have an obvious problem and I decide not to buy, the seller pays for the exam. If the doctor recommends more testing, then it is

Causes of Clear Clutches

Even if the birds are not damaging the eggs, consistently clear clutches indicate trouble. The "trouble" can be
• Infertility
• Disease
• Lack of bonding
• Old age

time to negotiate who pays for what. This technique probably automatically screens out dishonest people who are trying to pawn off sick or elderly parrots. Of course, this approach will not work if you are trying to buy long-distance. In that situation, steer clear of anyone who cannot produce verifiable references or copies of health records.

Breeding Loans

When you consider the cash outlay necessary to set up a pair of birds, searching for ways to save a few dollars is only natural. If you have a single parrot that you'd like to set up but can't find or can't afford a mate for it, you might be tempted to consider a breeder loan arrangement. In breeder loans, two people agree to place their birds together while each retains ownership. For example, if you own a female scarlet macaw but do not have the space or money to acquire a male, you might find another breeder who will place your hen with his or her male, and the two of you will split the money if

A proven pair of birds will incubate their eggs and care for their chicks.

and when the birds produce chicks. Where the birds are housed, who pays for what, and how the profits are split are all issues that need to be discussed carefully before you proceed. You should have a written contract that outlines each particular point of your agreement before the birds meet, or you could wind up losing your bird. If your potential partner balks at signing a contract, you should not proceed.

In my experience, breeding loans can be problematic, even with a written contract. A good friend of mine once had a male Amazon on loan, with a written contract that stated she would keep the birds in her aviary and she and her partner would split the proceeds from the chicks 50/50, less a small monthly maintenance fee for the cost of food and upkeep. A few months after they made the agreement, she discovered that her partner had moved and left no forwarding address or phone number, apparently abandoning his bird. In the meantime, his bird developed some health problems and ran up a fairly sizeable veterinary bill. Because of these problems, the pair produced only infertile eggs.

Four years later, my friend's "partner" suddenly phoned her and asked for his bird back. She explained that she had considered the bird abandoned after four years of no contact, but she was willing to return it providing he lived up to their written contract. When she told him that he owed her several hundred dollars for the monthly maintenance fee and veterinary bills, he became nasty and threatening, and he refused to pay. He then called the police and reported that she had stolen his bird. Even though she had a clearly worded and signed contract, her only recourse was to hire a lawyer and waste time and money in a civil court. All this for a bird that was infertile to boot!

Of course, not all breeding loans turn out so poorly. However, I've seen enough trouble caused to make me very, very cautious about recommending such an agreement. In the long run, doing what is necessary to buy a mate for your bird is almost always cheaper and smarter than putting yourself into a potentially bad situation. If you honestly feel a breeding loan is your best choice and you have complete trust in the other person, then go ahead. However, get everything in writing.

Chapter Four

Housing: Building a Better Birdhouse

There is a simple truism about breeding parrots—they will not produce unless they are happy and secure. Improper caging can be a major factor in breeding failures, yet it is usually one of the most overlooked problems. You must also be certain that the cage design works well for you. Otherwise, you will curse it every time you struggle with unwieldy locks, sticking trays, or hard-to-clean nooks and crannies. Caging mistakes are costly and frustrating. Therefore, spending a little time doing your homework now might save you lots of time and money down the road.

Before you begin, you must first decide where you're going to put the birds. If you live in a warm climate and have enough land, you might decide to build outdoor flights. If you live in a cold northern climate or if you are confined to a small suburban lot, then the birds will most likely be in cages in your house. Either way, you should carefully consider where you're going to place the cages for optimum safety and convenience.

The Great Outdoors

Under the right conditions, outdoor flights are wonderful. The birds have the benefit of fresh air and sunshine. Usually there's enough space to allow for larger cages than are practical indoors. Unfortunately, they are also more vulnerable to predators, thieves, and complaining neighbors in addition to various diseases carried by native wildlife. Before you decide to set up outdoor cages, you should consider several points:

• Do local zoning regulations allow you to keep parrots on your property? Are there any restrictions or building requirements?

• Do you have neighbors nearby who might object to the noise? Many breeders have lost court battles (and their birds) due to noise-pollution statutes.

• Can you provide foolproof security against thieves? Exotic bird theft is a huge and growing problem in many areas of the country.

• Can you properly protect against predators such as hawks, raccoons, coyotes, and feral dogs and cats?

Well-designed outdoor flights provide protection and shelter for the birds no matter what the weather conditions.

Beyond Closed Doors

Of course, keeping parrots indoors isn't without problems, either. Lack of space, poor ventilation, and inadequate lighting are just a few of the challenges indoor breeders face. You will want to consider the following questions:
• Is the space I have allocated large enough to house the birds without crowding?
• How will the noise level affect my quality of life? Can soundproofing materials be added to the room?
• Can I provide adequate ventilation and purification to maintain good air quality?
• Are there any windows to allow natural light to enter the area? Can I provide the necessary full-spectrum artificial light needed to make up for the lack of natural sunlight?
• Can I provide proper heating and cooling as needed?

Once you're comfortable with your decision about where to keep the birds, the next step is deciding the type and size of enclosure you'll keep them in.

• Can you provide adequate protection from the weather, including storms and flooding?
• Will you have easy access to water and electricity?

If you're in doubt about any of these questions, then do not proceed. At best, the problems you might encounter will be a terrible nuisance. At worst, they will cost your birds their lives.

Cage Sizing

The outdoor breeders and the indoor folks often disagree about what constitutes proper cage sizing. For example, some people will claim that macaws need to be kept in huge flight cages at least 20 feet

(6 m) long in order to breed. Other folks insist that their macaws breed happily in a small, wrought-iron cage in the family living room.

The truth is that there is no single right answer, no simple formula, to determine proper cage sizing. In general, "the bigger, the better" is the usual rule for cage sizing. However, the most important measure of suitability is how your birds act in the cage. If they seem restless, irrita-

Caging Requirements

To determine if your cage is the right size, ask yourself the following questions:
• Do the birds have plenty of room to move about freely and flap their wings?
• Is the cage large enough to allow more than one perch to be placed inside?
• Is there enough space to put toys into the cage without overcrowding?
• Do the birds have enough room to get away from each other if they begin to get on each other's nerves?

If you could not answer *yes* to each of these questions, then the cage is wrong. Never, under any circumstances, attempt to keep a pair of birds in a cage that is too small. They will suffer both physically and emotionally from the stress and from the lack of room to exercise. If you do not have the space, then do not keep the species!

ble, or spend an inordinate amount of time hanging on the bars, it might very well be too small. If they huddle in a far corner and seem fearful or nervous, the cage may be too large and open, and they feel vulnerable as a result.

As a rule of thumb, a cage for a single pet parrot should be at least one and a half times the width of the bird's wingspan. Therefore, a bird that has a wingspan of 16 inches (40 cm) should be in a cage at least 24 inches (60 cm) wide. This is a minimum recommendation. In most cases, bigger is better. Of course, when you put two birds into the cage, it needs to be roughly twice as large to provide both birds with suitable room. Active species, such as cockatoos and caiques, might need even more space. On the other hand, some African parrots seem to feel insecure in large cages and might do better in a slightly smaller enclosure. Once again, knowing your birds is important. Be honest when evaluating their needs.

Cage Types and Materials

Although an in-depth discussion of how to build cages and aviaries is beyond the scope of this book, I'd like to cover some basics about design and construction to help you get started. To a large degree, the species you have chosen will dictate the cage construction. Obviously, you cannot keep macaws in an enclosure made from wood and fine netting (at least not for very long!), and small parrots can squeeze right through the large weave of chain-link. The wire gauge, bar spacing, and design are just as important as overall size for the safety and comfort of your birds. In general, there are three basic types of breeder enclosures: traditional cages, suspended cages, and flight cages.

Traditional Cages

Traditional cages are the usual birdcages you find in pet stores and mail-order catalogs. They are available in a wide variety of sizes, materials, and finishes. Some of them are even designed with a small extra door on the side panel to accommodate a nest box. If you're planning to keep small-to-medium-sized parrots in an indoor setting, these cages can be an excellent choice. Most common are the powder-coated wrought-iron or plated-wire styles,

An indoor bird room should include plenty of light, good ventilation, and enough space for appropriately sized cages.

although stainless steel and acrylic models are also available. Do not use acrylic since it scratches, dulls, and yellows easily and it does not allow the birds to climb naturally. Stainless steel is absolutely wonderful, but it is very expensive. If you can afford it, you'll love its durability and ease of cleaning. Wrought iron or high-quality plated wire are a little more affordable and hold up fairly well. Avoid the inexpensive wire cages with plastic bottoms, however, since these types usually do not stand up to much wear and tear.

When buying a traditional cage, keep in mind that most styles are designed with pet birds in mind. They might have features that are unnecessary or inconvenient for breeding birds. For example, many wrought-iron styles have fancy playpen tops and elaborate seed aprons that add greatly to the price. Check to see if the manufacturer has a similar design without those features. If so, you'll likely save some money.

Whichever style you choose, buy a good-quality cage from a reputable manufacturer. Bargain cages are often a headache waiting to happen, especially when shoddy parts wear out and you find that replacements are not available. The same goes for buying used cages. If it is going to need replacement parts, do not buy it until you can identify and contact the manufacturer. Even if parts are available, you might be stunned at the price. Not uncommonly, a tray and grate cost 20 to 25

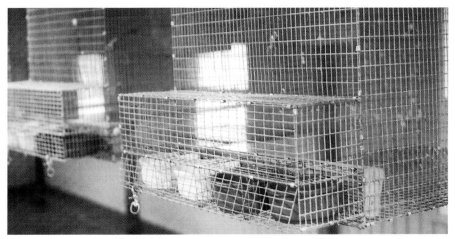
Suspended cages can be used indoors or out and are easy to maintain.

percent of the price of a whole new cage. Do your homework before you make a costly mistake. Besides, used cages can be a great source of disease transmission. If the previous occupants died from an infectious disease, remember that you will most likely be bringing those pathogens home along with the cage. *Never* bring a used cage onto your premises until it is carefully and thoroughly disinfected (which is not an easy job on an object as large as a cage).

Suspended Cages

Suspended cages are a popular choice among parrot breeders because they are inexpensive and easy to maintain. These cages are constructed from wire mesh and, as the name indicates, are suspended above the ground. Suspended cages can be placed onto wooden frames or mounted to fence posts

outside or can be hung from ceiling joists indoors. Because the cage bottom is just mesh, droppings and scattered foods fall through, where they can be swept up or hosed down without opening the cage and disturbing the birds. These cages are usually home-built, although a few supply companies sell finished models. The mesh size and wire gauge will depend on the species you intend to keep, but you should keep a few points in mind. Always be certain to use a sturdy enough wire, or you will find that your birds bend and break it to escape. With wire gauge, the smaller the number, the heavier the wire. For example, 20 gauge is thin and could be bent easily between your fingers, while 10 gauge is heavy and rigid. It would require a sturdy pair of pliers to bend at all.

In general, 0.5 inch by 1 inch (1.3 cm by 2.5 cm) 16-gauge wire will

Mesh size and wire gauge will depend on the species you intend to keep.

work fine for most small-to-medium parrots. However, 0.5 inch or 1 inch by 1 inch (1.3 cm or 2.5 cm by 2.5 cm) 14-gauge will hold medium and some larger species. For large birds that are voracious chewers (such as Moluccan cockatoos and most macaws), you will need to use 12.5 gauge 1 inch by 1 inch (2.5 cm by 2.5 cm). Hyacinth and large green-wing macaws might require 9-inch wire in 2-inch by 2-inch (5-cm by 5-cm) squares. For outdoor use, the smaller 0.5-inch by 1-inch (1.3-cm by 2.5-cm) squares will help keep wild birds, snakes, and rats from entering the cage to steal food and will make it more difficult for predators to reach in and grab the parrots. However, do not use 0.5-inch (1.3 cm) spacing on cockatoos and macaws even if it is heavy-duty wire. They will happily destroy the cage by grabbing two bars and crimping them together in their beak until the welds break. Wider spacing of 1 inch to 2 inches (2.5 cm to 5 cm) will quickly foil that game.

When using these cages outdoors, you will need to build a roof to shelter the birds from harsh sunlight, weather, and predators. Some people cover just the area over the food dishes and nest box, leaving the rest uncovered so that the birds can enjoy some sunshine and rain showers. In certain areas of the country, however, large numbers of parrots have died from *Sarcocystis*, a protozoal parasite that is carried in

Large outdoor flight cages allow the birds to fly and exercise.

the feces of opossums. By placing a roof over the entire cage, opossums cannot climb across the top and defecate into the cage. Of course, insects that have come into contact with the feces can still spread this deadly parasite. However, covering the cage and maintaining good sanitation will offer some degree of protection.

Joel Murphy, a veterinarian and aviculturist in Florida, recommends surrounding outdoor cages with an enclosure of 0.25-inch (0.6-cm) hardware cloth topped by heavy-duty mosquito netting. This will not only keep out most insects and vermin, but it will temporarily keep in any bird that manages to escape from its cage. Parrots can (and do)

escape with alarming frequency. Having some sort of safety barrier set up around your cages is important. Most breakouts happen when you open the door to service the cage or catch a bird. Even a tent of poultry netting draped completely around the cages will at least slow down the escapee and perhaps allow you time to catch the bird before it escapes completely.

Flight Cages

Flight cages can be made of the same materials as suspended cages. However, flights extend to the ground and are usually larger. Parrot flights look much like covered dog kennels. In fact, I use premade chain-link dog kennel panels to house my large macaws. Because these birds are indoors, the panels are set directly onto a tiled floor in the bird room, and the top is covered with another panel. The flights are 6 feet (1.8 m) high so I can step right inside to sweep and mop the floor. For less than $300, I have a sturdy, easy-to-maintain cage, although my neighbors have probably questioned my decorating style since they saw me carrying chain-link fencing *into* the house.

Of course, outdoor flights are not as simple. Ideally, the base should be made of concrete, with a slight slope to facilitate drainage. If you cannot create a concrete base, then the wire must be buried several inches into the ground to keep predators out and birds in. Many species of parrots are quite adept at digging (especially cockatoos). They will merrily tunnel their way to freedom unless the wire is well buried. Allow at least 4 inches (10 cm) between flights so that the birds cannot fight with their neighbors. Some species, such as Amazons, might even require visual barriers between flights or they will not breed. Of course, the need for roofing and safety nets is the same for flights as it is for suspended cages.

Heavy-duty chain-link panels can be used to construct cages for large macaws and cockatoos.

Allow at least 4 inches (10 cm) between flights to prevent fighting between neighboring pairs.

The Zinc Controversy

One final issue about cages requires a little discussion. In recent years, some veterinarians have raised the question about the safety of zinc in caging materials. Although trace amounts of dietary zinc are necessary for life, excess amounts of this heavy metal are toxic and can result in lethargy, depression, and death. The coating on most galvanized wire used to construct cages contains 98 percent or more zinc. Birds that spend a lot of time chewing on the wire can develop zinc toxicosis, also known as new-wire disease. Scrubbing the wire thoroughly with a vinegar solution will remove most (but not all) of the free zinc and limit the amount that can be easily ingested. Even traditional pet birdcages often contain zinc in their coatings, although usually at much lower levels than galvanized wire. Zinc shows up in the hardware and chain on many bird toys and can be found in some rubber and plastic.

The controversy lies in what, if any, level of zinc should be tolerated as safe. On one side of the debate are those folks who believe that any environmental source of zinc is dangerous. On the other side are those who, while they acknowledge the very real danger of zinc toxicosis from cheap or improperly prepped wire, feel it is unlikely that a bird could ingest excess zinc from a properly cleaned, good-quality wire. In truth, no one really knows the answer. Some birds do show high blood levels of the metal, which drop when they're placed into zinc-free environments. Yet other birds kept in galvanized cages show completely normal blood levels, even if they spend a lot of time chewing the wire.

When this issue first arose, I was immediately worried about my macaws. As I said earlier, I keep them in galvanized chain link, and they spend a great deal of their day attempting to unravel the links and break off the ties. I rushed them to my veterinarian for blood tests and was relieved when the results came back normal. I then brought in a pet cockatoo that was housed in a high-quality, powder-coated, wrought-iron cage. This bird is not a chewer and never spent any time mouthing the bars. Her tests showed elevated zinc levels, although she showed no signs of illness and was in perfect feather condition.

I'm not a scientist but I suspect that there is more to the zinc issue than meets the eye. Most nutrients in the body work synergistically with each other to remain in balance, so a deficiency of one creates an excess of the other. Copper works this way with zinc. An excess of zinc can create a copper deficiency, but can a dietary deficiency of copper cause high blood levels of zinc? Of course, these are questions for veterinarians and researchers. I'm certainly not recommending supplementing any other trace elements to your bird's diet. The point I am trying to make is that, until we have some definitive answers on the subject, I think it's too early to draw broad conclusions about the relative safety of zinc-coated cages.

Big differences exist in the quality and safety of wire, depending on the manufacturer. Therefore, buy only from sources that sell high-quality wire intended for use by exotic birds. If you have any concerns, discuss the matter with your avian veterinarian or get your birds tested. Unfortunately, if you suspect a problem, very few options exist for large suspended or flight cages that are zinc free.

Outfitting the Cage

Once you've decided on a cage, the next step is to choose the proper accessories to create a comfortable and safe environment for your birds and an easy-to-maintain routine for you. Some people pay little attention to cage accessories like perches and cups. However, these simple items can have a surprisingly large impact on health and productivity.

Perches

Since adult parrots do not lie down (unless they are playing or sick), they are on their feet 24 hours a day for life. Therefore, they should have a variety of comfortable perches in different sizes and materials to keep their feet healthy and well exercised. A parrot with just one smooth, uniform perch will likely develop pressure sores on its feet and hocks. What might not be so obvious, however, is that unsuitable perches can also result in breeding failures and infertile eggs. If the birds are not able to get a steady, solid grip during mating, fertilization might not occur.

When I first began breeding birds, it was my dream to raise green-winged macaws. I was discouraged, however, by stories about how difficult they were to breed. Many people told me that they would produce eggs readily, but the eggs were often infertile. I asked my avian veterinarian, who is quite an authority on parrot reproduction, for his opinion. He said that he had seen lots of infertility in green-wings, but he felt most of it was caused by poor perch choices. He explained that these heavy-bodied parrots have difficulty maintaining proper balance during mating and suggested placing two perches parallel to each other about 20 inches (50 cm) apart in the cage. I did just that, and my green-wings produced chicks on their first attempt. I've had the pair for five years. They go to nest twice a year like clockwork, each time making beautiful babies. I've often seen them mating. The female always stands on one perch, then leans forward and grasps the other perch with her beak to steady herself. Perhaps it's just a coincidence, and they might have had fertile eggs without the second perch. However, I'm not going to remove it and find out!

There are now a wide variety of perch materials available. I usually supply my birds with one or two natural hardwood perches, such as manzanita or ribbon wood. These are easy to clean and hard to chew. The natural variations in shape and thickness help exercise the feet. I also like to offer one of the cement or terra-cotta pedicure perches that help trim the nails and beak. Some people worry that the rough texture of these perches will be too harsh on a bird's feet. On the contrary, I find that my birds really seem to like these perches and will gladly sleep on them if they are placed into a high corner of the cage. The heavy texture probably gives them a good, no-slip grip for sleeping.

For heavy chewers, you can also fashion a chew-proof perch out of PVC pipe. Although this is durable and easy to clean, it tends to be slippery. If you decide to use this, take a coarse file to the surface and rough it up as much as possible. Because it has a smooth and uniform surface, do not use it as the only perch in a cage. Again, the birds need some variety to stay comfortable.

The one perch material you should not use is rope. Rope is fine as a secondary perch for pet birds that are monitored closely, but it has too many drawbacks to recommend it for breeding pairs. To begin with, it soils easily and is difficult to clean. The only way really to clean it properly is to remove it from the cage and run it through the dishwasher, which means disturbing the pair each time you want to get the gunk off. It also frays easily. You run the risk that the birds will become entangled and lose a toe, break a leg, or worse. Trust me; I've had to untangle an angry and frightened parrot from a rope perch, and it was no fun for either of us. Besides, these perches are too bouncy and flexible. If the birds try to use one during mating, they will probably not be successful. Stick with solid, non-slip wood or concrete, and you'll eliminate at least one of the possible causes of infertility.

Food Dishes

Once the cage is properly fitted with perches, next you'll need to consider the food bowls. The size, material, and style will depend a great deal on the species you're breeding. However, you should follow some general guidelines. First of all, choose the appropriate size. Do not buy huge food and water bowls for small parrots, or they'll most likely use them as sandboxes and swimming pools. Don't think that you will have to fill them less often. Food and water *must be changed daily* or you run the risk of poisoning your birds with bacteria and fungi from spoiled food and soiled water. Too-large dishes are simply a waste. On the other hand, do not buy small dishes for large parrots. They won't hold enough food and water, and the birds will most likely use them as toys. Crock flinging is an Olympic sport for most large parrots. Small, lightweight dishes do not offer much of a challenge.

Once you've figured out the appropriate size, you'll need to decide on what type of material to buy. Bird dishes are available in plastic, metal, or ceramic. Once again, your choice will depend on the species. Plastic can be fine for most small and some medium parrots, but the bigger guys will chew it to pieces. Even some small parrots can be destructive chewers. I have a large number of the *Poicephalus* species (Senegals, Meyers, and brown headed), which are stocky little parrots about 10 inches (25 cm) tall. They can destroy plastic dishes faster than birds twice their size. Plastic also stains pretty easily, so it's not usually a good first choice.

Ceramic crocks are great, but they are breakable. Some birds will pick them up and toss them around until they shatter. If you can purchase a style that is too heavy for your birds to lift, then these are a good choice. Keep in mind that once the glaze is chipped or deeply scratched, bacteria and other nasty organisms can thrive in the porous ceramic. Replace damaged crocks as often as necessary. Always buy from a reputable manufacturer. Do not ever use decorative crocks that are not approved for food usage. Certain types of inexpensive, imported glazed pottery can contain high amounts of lead and other heavy metals in the glaze. To be on the safe side, never leave highly acidic foods or liquids (such as juice) in a ceramic crock. Acid can cause any lead that is present to leach out. Never use the galvanized coop-cup type bowls that are commonly available from farm and poultry suppliers since these are a likely source of zinc, lead, and other heavy-metal contamination.

My personal favorite for food and water dishes is stainless steel. It's lightweight, extremely durable, non-reactive, and easy to clean and disinfect. Unfortunately, because it's so lightweight, the birds will toss it unless you can lock it down somehow. My cages are designed with dish holders that the bowls slide into so that they can't be dumped. A few good styles of self-locking bowls are also on the market. If all else fails, I've successfully used the large spring clamps available at any hardware store to fasten the bowls securely to the cage bars.

Of course, if you really want to outwit a water dumper, you can switch to water bottles. Most parrots make the transition to bottles pretty easily. However, I suggest you continue to offer water in a bowl until you're certain that the birds have figured out how to drink from the bottle. For parrots, always use the heavy-duty, professional-style bottles with guards and stainless-steel tubes. The cheap plastic or thin glass styles on the market for dogs or small animals aren't suitable for parrots. Parrots will quickly detach or destroy them. I've used water bottles with varying degrees of success. They're fine for most birds, but some treat them as toys. Some birds learn to push the little ball valve up with their toenail while the water drains out all over the floor. Cockatoos are notorious for stuffing bits of food into the tubes and clog-

These food and water dishes slide into a wire box that prevents the birds from lifting the dishes out and flinging them around.

ging them up. If you decide to go this route, rinse and refill the bottles with clean water every day. Make certain that the tube is not blocked and the water is flowing properly.

Nest Boxes

The final step in outfitting a breeder cage is setting up the nest box. Nest boxes come in a variety of sizes and configurations, depending on the species. They are most commonly made of wood, but galvanized metal is often used for large, voracious chewers. They come in various styles.

Rectangle ones are usually small wooden boxes in sizes for parakeets, cockatiels, lovebirds, and other small parrots.

Grandfather refers to a tall vertical box in a shape reminiscent of a grandfather clock. These common boxes are popular for many small-to-medium parrots, such as Amazons, conures, Pionus parrots, and others.

Horizontal style is similar to a grandfather box, only it's hung horizontally. This style seems to be preferred by most macaws and some cockatoos (especially Goffin's).

T-boxes are T-shaped, have two entrance holes, and are used primarily for cockatoos. Cockatoos have a predisposition toward mate aggression when breeding, and sometimes the hens are killed or injured by the males. This style of box makes it difficult for an angry male to trap the hen inside since she can exit one hole as he enters the other.

Boot (or L) boxes are a popular style for nervous or high-strung parrots, such as African greys. Greys have a tendency to leap wildly into their nest boxes when people enter the room. With the traditional vertical grandfather boxes, the birds often

Wooden nest boxes come in a variety of sizes.

land on their eggs and crack them. In boot boxes, the eggs are usually laid in the protected toe of the boot, so accidentally scrambled eggs are not as likely to occur.

Barrels: For the large macaws, oak whiskey barrels, 55-gallon (200-L) drums, and large galvanized garbage cans can be turned into simple and effective nest boxes. I've been using 30-gallon (115-L) galvanized cans for my macaws for years, and they seem to love them. They're inexpensive, lightweight, and easy to replace when they begin to rust. Just wire the lid closed, turn the can onto its side, and cut a 4-inch (10-cm) square entrance hole in the side. Crimp over the cut edges so there are no sharp spots. Then, drill two small holes at either end for hanging. Use clothesline hooks, which are shaped like huge cup hooks and have a threaded end. You can bolt these through the drilled holes and bend them as necessary to make the can hang properly. The lid (which is now on the side) serves as an inspection door.

Other designs and alternatives for nest boxes are on the market, but these are the most commonly available types. You might need to experiment a little to see which style your birds prefer. One word of caution. If you are breeding outdoors, be certain that the nest box is shielded as much as possible from direct sunlight, *especially* if you use metal boxes. These can rapidly turn into ovens in the hot sun and kill chicks and developing eggs.

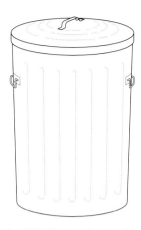

30-gallon (114-L) galvanized garbage can

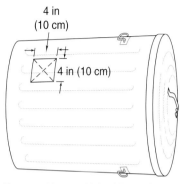

4 in
(10 cm)

4 in (10 cm)

Turn on side, cut "X" in side as shown.

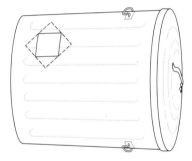

Fold over cut sections and crimp tightly so there are no sharp edges. You should now have a 4-inch (10-cm) square hole.

Tools Needed:
- ✓ 1 - 30-gallon (114-L) galvanized can with lid
- ✓ 2 - Clothesline hangers with 4 nuts and large washers
- ✓ Wire
- ✓ Drill
- ✓ Wire shears
- ✓ Pliers

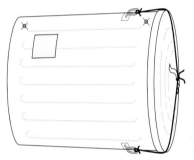

Drill holes at X's. Put clothesline hanger through holes, secure with nut and washers. Wire the can handles to lid to prevent it from popping open. Can is now ready to hang on cage. Lid can be opened when you want to inspect box.

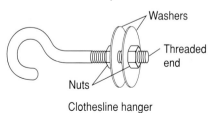

Washers

Threaded end

Nuts

Clothesline hanger

This is an easy and inexpensive method for constructing macaw nest boxes. The design can be adapted to 55-gallon (209-L) drums for hyacinth macaws.

This *Eclectus* parrot enjoys a uniquely designed nest box that imitates a natural tree cavity.

Substrates

What you put into the nest box is just as critical as the style of box you choose. A suitable substrate should be reasonably soft to cushion the eggs, resistant to mold and bacteria, and digestible in case the chicks swallow any. Pine shavings are probably the most commonly used material. Unfortunately, they are not digestible. Many years ago, I lost a chick to an impaction of pine shavings in its gizzard. I now use sterilized fir bark chunks, which are commonly sold as a terrarium litter for iguanas and other reptiles. This bark is very soft and does a beautiful job of cushioning the eggs and maintaining humidity. The chunks are too large for a chick to swallow. When the adult birds chew it, it breaks down to the consistency of fine saw-dust, which should pass easily through a chick's system without impacting. As with any substrate, it needs to be changed after each clutch or more often as necessary.

Environmental Considerations

Now that you've gotten the breeding cage completely set up, the time has come to take a look at the overall environment. If your cages are outdoors, be certain that the birds have sufficient shelter and privacy. Planting small trees and shrubs around the flights will offer some protection from wind and weather and will enhance the feeling of security. Although natural sunlight is certainly beneficial, make sure that the birds have some shaded areas to escape the direct harsh rays and avoid overheating. For indoor parrots that do not have the benefit of sunlight, the need for supplemental lighting is crucial to maintain health and fertility.

The Right Light

Although people tend to take it for granted, most organisms require light to survive and prosper. Vitamin synthesis, growth and reproductive hormones, and brain chemicals are all affected by light. Unfortunately, regular indoor artificial lighting is vastly inferior to natural sunlight. All light is composed of different wavelengths, ranging from ultraviolet through the visible spectrum and on through infrared. Ordinary incandescent light contains almost no ultraviolet rays and is lacking in the blue end of the spectrum. Regular fluorescent tubes are a little better but still differ quite a bit from sunlight. Placing your birds near windows will not solve the problem since plain window glass screens out approximately 99 percent of the ultraviolet end of the spectrum. Just as the wrong kinds of food will cause a vitamin deficiency, the wrong kinds of light will cause a light deficiency. Light deficiencies can negatively affect almost every bodily function, causing both physical and emotional illnesses.

To prevent problems of this sort, you must provide full-spectrum lighting for your indoor birds. Full-spectrum bulbs are designed to duplicate the range of natural sunlight closely. Although they are more expensive than regular lightbulbs, the difference in productivity and health will more than make up for the cost. Although they are most commonly available as fluorescent tubes, a few varieties of full-spectrum incandescents are on the market now. While either style will work, you will need to place the lights very close to the birds (preferably no

more than 2 or 3 feet [60 or 90 cm] from the cage) to gain the maximum benefit. Also, some brands do not guarantee to maintain the full spectrum for the life of the bulb. Look for brands that do maintain the spectrum, or replace the bulbs as recommended by the manufacturer. By manipulating the amount of time the lights are on during the day, you can stimulate breeding in some species.

Over the winter months, I usually keep the lights on for only about 10 hours a day. During this time, my winter-breeding Africans go to nest, but the rest of the birds take a break. As springtime approaches, I gradually extend the artificial daylight to about 14 or 15 hours. This increase in day length stimulates the Amazons and most of my other species to begin breeding. Interestingly, my large macaws seem unaffected by day length and will breed whenever they darn well feel like it, no matter what the lighting conditions of the moment. I've had macaw chicks in the dead of winter and during the dog days of summer. You might need to experiment for a few seasons to see what works for the species you keep. In any case, do not ever provide your birds with less than 10 hours a day of light. And never extend the day period beyond 16 hours, or their health might suffer.

Chapter Five

Basic Breeding Supplies (Batteries Not Included)

When I first began breeding parrots, I was totally unprepared for all the *stuff* I needed to get, and I spent many frantic moments trying to track down the necessary supplies in a hurry. Careful preparation is expensive. However, attempting to raise birds without the proper equipment is almost guaranteed to fail. If you do your shopping in advance, you'll never have the heartbreak of losing a chick that could have been easily saved if only you had had the right tools.

Incubators

Incubators are specialized heating units designed to hatch eggs. Some parrots (especially young or inexperienced pairs) will lay fertile eggs but refuse to sit on them. When this happens, you'll need a method of artificial incubation. While fostering the abandoned eggs under another hen is occasionally possible, this is tricky at best. It usually is not

feasible in a small breeding operation with limited pairs. The best solution is an egg incubator. Dozens of styles are available. Be aware that many have been designed for hatching poultry and game birds. When choosing an incubator, you must purchase only a model that has been designed and tested for exotic birds. Developing eggs need to be rotated several times a day so that the growing embryo doesn't stick to the inner membrane and die, but parrot embryos are extremely fragile compared with domestic poultry. The egg-turning mechanisms on many poultry incubators are rolling bars, which can kill parrot embryos with their harsh vibrations. Most exotic bird incubators have rocking trays that turn the eggs very gently without vibration. Do not try to save money by buying a model without an automatic egg turner unless you plan on remaining home during the entire incubation period (typically 23 to 31 days) so that you can manually rotate the eggs the necessary 20 or

so times a day. Automatic egg turn-
ers are well worth any added cost.

You must choose a forced-air,
rather than a still-air, model. This
simply means that the unit has a fan
that circulates the heat, which
reduces gradients in temperature
and humidity. Still-air models work
fine for chickens and ducks, but parrot eggs seem to require the more
uniform conditions in a forced-air
model. Make sure that the brand
you choose has a very reliable thermometer for measuring temperature
and a good wet-bulb thermometer
for calculating humidity. Inexpensive
temperature/humidity gauges are
not accurate enough for egg incubation. Most quality incubators have
digital or analog temperature read-
outs and rely on the wet-bulb thermometer to gauge humidity. Chapter
Nine will discuss this in more detail,
but be aware that these are features
to look for when choosing a model.

First-time incubator buyers are
often confused about the need for
humidity control devices. Although
some rather expensive devices are
on the market that will monitor and
automatically adjust the humidity levels, most common brands rely on a
simple system of water reservoirs
and vents. To increase humidity, you
add more water or partially close the
vent. To decrease humidity, you open
the vent wider. Although parrot eggs
require precise humidity levels, these
simple vent systems work quite well,
provided you monitor them occasionally during the day. Unless you are
dealing with extremely valuable, rare,

*Choose an incubator that has been
designed to hatch parrot eggs.*

or difficult-to-hatch species, you
probably don't need to shell out
the money for automatic humidity
controls.

Another nice feature to look for is
high/low temperature alarms. In the
event of a malfunction, these units
will beep loudly or sound an alarm to
let you know that the temperature
has strayed more than a few degrees
from where it was set. This is an
important safety feature, which will
allow you to rescue the eggs before
they are cooked or fatally chilled.

To incubate eggs successfully,
you will also need a separate hatching unit. Eggs nearing hatch have

different requirements than eggs in earlier stages of development, so one incubator will not work for both. Although you can buy actual hatching units, you should purchase a second incubator instead. Any incubator can be turned into a hatcher by shutting off the automatic egg turner and increasing the humidity (see Chapter Nine). By purchasing two incubators, you can use one as a hatcher, but you'll also have a back-up incubator in case one breaks down. I have an expensive, high-quality incubator that I use for newly developing eggs and a less expensive (but still good-quality) incubator that I use mostly as a hatching unit.

For a good-quality forced-air parrot incubator with automatic egg turning, expect to spend anywhere from $275 to $1,500, depending on the model and features you choose. Several nice ones are on the market from manufacturers such as Humidaire, Grumbach, Brinsea, and Lyon Electric. (See "Resource Guide" for contact information).

Brooders

Brooders are heating units similar to incubators except they're designed for warming chicks, not eggs. Baby parrots are altricial, which means they're born naked (or with sparse down), blind, and completely helpless. Poultry chicks, on the other hand, are precocial, which means they pop out of their shells with eyes open, a full covering of fluffy down, and are ready to walk around and eat on their own. Parrot chicks need to be kept on supplemental heat until they're almost fully feathered. The younger the chick, the more critical and precise its temperature and humidity requirements.

You can choose from many different styles of parrot brooders, from fancy professional units to homemade designs. The best are designed much like incubators, with forced air, air filtration, temperature alarms, and precision temperature controls. Most of these are stationary units. A few portable models are on the market, and these are indispensable if you ever need to travel with the babies. Because I work full-time, I need to bring my young chicks to work with me to hand-feed during the day. I have a few portable brooders that plug into my car's cigarette lighter to operate while I'm driving and then plug into an adapter that converts them to regular household current when I arrive at the office. I live in Chicago, and these wonderful units allow me to transport even fragile, one-day-old chicks safely during savage, below-zero winter weather.

For older chicks, temperature control is not quite as critical. You can safely design a makeshift brooder out of a simple glass aquarium. Begin by choosing an appropriately sized tank. Usually a 10- to 20-gallon (40- to 75-L) size is sufficient for small-to-medium parrots. Line the tank with a safe bedding material for the babies, such as paper towels or cloth diapers. Do not use pine shavings or other litters because the chicks may very possibly pick at the litter and ingest it. Besides, these grow bacteria rapidly and usually do not offer solid enough footing to support a chick's legs. You can use paper towels for smaller species and cloth diapers or terry cloth bath towels for the larger birds. Do not use terry cloth for young chicks or smaller species because they tend to get their toes tangled in the fabric loops. This is not usually a problem with the big guys, however. The thickness of the towels gives them a nice firm footing, which helps prevent splayed legs.

Once you have set up the tank, you can use several different methods to supply heat. The easiest and least expensive method is to use either an undertank heater designed for reptiles or a human heating pad. Undertank heaters are thin, plastic pads that stick to the outside bottom of the tank. They have heating elements built in, which will provide a gentle radiant heat through the glass. If you use one of these, buy one that covers only about half of the tank so that the chick can move to the cooler side if it becomes too warm. Always keep a layer of bedding on the tank floor so that the baby is not in direct contact with the heated glass. Place an easy-to-read thermometer inside so that you can monitor the temperature. You can then control the temperature a bit by covering the top of the tank with a towel. If it's too cool, cover the entire top. If it's too warm, pull back the

A small aquarium draped with a heating pad can serve as a brooder for older chicks.

towel to let more air in. Keep in mind that this makeshift arrangement is *only* for older chicks that just require a little supplemental heat. Never use a homemade brooder like this for new hatchlings since maintaining the precise temperature that young babies require is nearly impossible.

You can also use a heating pad instead of the undertank heater, but place it on top of the tank, not under it. Heating pads give off more heat. Sandwiching it under the tank could create a fire hazard. You can use screen covers on the tanks and place the heating pad across one half. The screen cover allows the heat to radiate down but prevents older babies from reaching up and trying to chew on the pad.

There are a few other options for a heat source, but they do not work as well. Some people use aquarium heaters immersed in a jug of water placed inside the tank. However, this method is clumsy and it does not always give off enough radiant heat when the room temperature is cool. You can also use ceramic heat disks that are made for reptiles and birds. These have a lightbulb-type base, but they emit no light, only heat. They can be screwed into a clamp-on light fixture and easily attached to the top of the tank. The drawback with these is that they become extremely hot and can cause severe burns if the chicks are able to reach up and touch them. They are also a fire hazard if they come into contact with combustible materials, so use these with caution.

Bulb Warning

Never, under any circumstances, use infrared heat bulbs anywhere near your parrots. Many of these bulbs are coated with Teflon, which, when exposed to high heat, gives off invisible, odorless fumes that are highly toxic to birds. These fumes will kill any birds in the vicinity, although humans are apparently not affected. Be extremely cautious about any heat source not intended for use around birds, since identifying which ones might contain Teflon is almost impossible.

For a professionally manufactured stationary or portable brooder, expect to spend between $250 and $600. An aquarium with a screen cover, undertank heater or heating pad, and thermometer/hygrometer will run about $50 to $75. Keep in mind that, unlike incubators, you'll probably need more than one brooder since chicks of different ages and different species should be housed separately. If you have multiple breeding pairs, you should begin with at least one stationary model, one portable model, and a few aquariums for older chicks. Some good manufacturers are Dean's Animal Supply, Petiatric Supply, and Brinsea. (See "Resource Guide.")

Hospital Cages

Hospital cages are similar to brooders but are intended for sick adult birds. You can use a regular brooder for this purpose. However, sometimes an adult parrot will escape from or damage a unit designed for chicks. If you do use a chick brooder for a sick adult, keep in mind that you must carefully and completely disinfect every inch of it before using it for babies again. Keeping a separate unit for use with sick birds is better, because the possibility of disease transmission is just too great. Some viruses are extremely hardy, and a piece of equipment as complicated as a brooder is difficult to disinfect completely.

A few professionally manufactured hospital cages are on the market, ranging from about $200 to $600. In most cases, however, you can get by with the makeshift setup described at right. Expect to spend about $50 to $250 for a small, sturdy extra cage, depending on the size you need for the species you breed. For medium-to-large parrots, inexpensive suitcase-style dog crates make a great temporary hospital cage and can be easily folded down for storage when not in use.

Weaning Cages

Folding dog crates also make good weaning cages for medium-to-large parrots. Weaning cages are simply transitional cages for baby birds that are old enough to perch and do not require supplemental heat but are too young to be placed into an adult cage. Although you can use regular birdcages for weaning, I prefer dog crates for a few reasons. As mentioned earlier, many varieties fold down for easy storage when not in use. Since they're so portable, they're easy to clean—just drag them into the backyard for a good scrubbing and hose them down. The shape is good, too. They usually have plenty of length for playing and flapping but not much height, which makes them perfect for chicks. Clumsy young parrots love to climb. However, they're not really good at it, so they fall a lot. By avoiding tall cages, you'll keep the falling distance to a minimum.

Construction Instructions

The simplest way to make a hospital cage is to take a small cage or carrier, cover the top and three sides with a towel or blanket (leave just the front open), and place a heating pad or two on top. Place the pad(s) onto one side only so the bird can move to a cooler spot if it becomes overheated. Make sure the cords do not rest against the cage where the bird can reach them. If it's likely to chew, place a piece of heavy screening or hardware cloth between the cage and the pad to prevent accidents. In general, a really sick parrot does not usually have the energy to chew and destroy things. Once it begins taking enough interest in the surroundings to notice chewable items, it has usually recovered enough that you can remove the heat source. Of course, *always* keep a sick bird carefully quarantined away from the rest of your flock and far away from your nursery area.

No matter what style cage you decide to use, place the perches low so that the chicks feel comfortable and can step on and off them easily. I usually place large, shallow crocks of water and weaning food onto the cage floor so the chicks can explore and play with the food without worrying about perching at the same time. If you breed different species that vary greatly in size, you'll need appropriate weaning cages for each size category. Folding dog crates sell for about $50 to $250, depending on the size and wire gauge and are readily available in most pet shops and mail-order pet catalogs.

Gram Scales

A good-quality gram scale is essential for tracking the growth and health of baby birds. Healthy parrot chicks grow by leaps and bounds. A young chick that is not gaining weight might be in serious trouble. Weighing your chicks every day (preferably in the morning and always with an empty crop) and keeping a log of their weights is important. Parrots are traditionally weighed in grams, not ounces, so be

A good-quality gram scale is an essential tool for raising chicks.

certain that the model you buy has the capacity to measure in grams.

Choosing a model that has a tare function is also helpful. The tare function allows you to place a bowl or small perch stand onto the scale platform, press a button that resets the scale to zero, and then place the chick into the bowl for weighing. This allows you to get an accurate weight without having to deduct the weight of the container or perch. Small kitchen or postal scales work great for birds, but spend enough money to get an accurate one. You'll want to pick a brand that has a capacity of up to 2,000 grams (about 4.4 pounds) and is accurate plus or minus 1 gram. Although this level of precision usually isn't necessary for weighing adult birds, many small parrot species hatch out weighing only 3 or 4 grams, so a less accurate scale is virtually worthless for such tiny chicks. Even the large macaws hatch out only around 20 to 25 grams, so any error larger than plus or minus 1 or 2 grams is unacceptable.

Most scales of this type sell for about $50 to $100. A few quality brands are Pelouze, Sunbeam, and Soehnle. You can find them in office supply stores, kitchen and chef outlets, and through mail-order bird catalogs.

Candling Lights

Candling lights are essential for checking the fertility and growth of eggs. As a fertile egg starts to develop, blood vessels begin to form, which are visible when a bright light is shined through the shell. This is called candling. Infertile (or clear) eggs show no such development and display just a yellowish glow when held to a light. Although candling eggs by holding them up near a lightbulb or flashlight is possible, it is a bad idea. For starters, light sources of that size are too diffuse and make it difficult to get a good look. Secondly, that method requires a lot of handling of the egg, and you can kill the embryo by excessive jarring. Finally, light sources such as regular lightbulbs throw off a lot of heat, and the resulting thermal stress can also kill the fragile embryo.

Specialized candling lights are much safer and easier to use. Several styles are on the market. However, they are all basically very tiny, very bright lights and will allow you to see inside the egg clearly. My personal favorite is a battery-operated, 25-inch-long (65-cm-long) bendable model, which permits you to examine the eggs right inside the nest box without handling or disturbing them. Of course, you'll have to coax the parents out of the box first. Otherwise, you're likely to have scrambled and cracked eggs when the pair attempts to defend their nest and mounts an attack.

Candling lights are available mostly by mail order and generally cost between $25 and $75. MDS and Brinsea are two companies that manufacture a few good styles.

Feeding Implements and Disinfectants

To feed the chicks, you'll need an assortment of syringes, pipettes, or spoons. You'll also need a variety of disinfectants to sanitize the feeding implements, incubators, brooders, and other objects the babies come into contact with. These are discussed in greater detail in Chapter Eleven, but be aware that you can expect to spend anywhere from $10 to $50 a month for disinfectants and disposable feeding implements. These items are mostly available through veterinarians and mail-order suppliers.

Observation Systems

Although observation systems are not an absolute necessity for breeding parrots, the information they provide is invaluable in many ways. You can use the cameras to watch newly setup pairs for signs of bonding or aggression or to monitor pairs on eggs to make sure they are in the box and (presumably) incubating properly. If one of the birds does not look quite right, you can turn the camera on it to watch closely for signs of illness. Attempting to make any of the above determinations is useless while you are in the room because parrots will stop fighting, try to hide signs of illness, or jump into the nest box when a human is present. As soon as you leave the room, they will go back to what they were doing before you entered. A good observation system will save you many hours of hiding behind doorways, trying to sneak a peek at what is really happening in there.

For many years, I used a system of low-light, miniature black-and-white cameras attached by cables to a small monitor. These setups are commonly sold as security cameras for shops and businesses and are widely available. The only drawback was the need to run the cable from my aviary to my kitchen, where I kept the monitor. Moving or repositioning cameras was also difficult because of the cables.

I recently switched to a wonderful system that uses tiny color cameras with wireless transmitters. The base receiver, which will allow you to switch between up to four cameras, has a small LCD screen. Alternatively, it can be plugged into a regular television set for large-screen birdie TV.

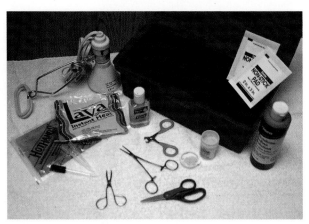

A well-stocked first-aid kit might save your bird's life.

Because the cameras are wireless, they can move around the aviary with ease. Most of these systems also allow you to record to a videocassette recorder if you are so inclined.

Expect to spend about $350 to $600 for a basic system with one camera. Extra cameras range from about $150 to $250. Several different brands are available at retail stores, including Sam's Club and Sharper Image stores nationwide.

Emergency and First-Aid Supplies

A well-stocked first-aid kit is perhaps one of the most important items to have if you keep birds. Parrots seem to spend a lot of time devising new and creative ways to hurt themselves, especially on holiday weekends when there isn't a veterinarian left in town. Although emergency first aid is no substitute for proper veterinary care, the necessary tools can often help you to stabilize the problem long enough to get professional help. Here is a brief rundown of the essentials.

• Clean towels for catching and restraining the injured bird.

• Gauze pads.

• Rolled gauze.

• Cotton balls and swabs.

• Small, fine-tipped artist's paintbrushes for repairing eggs.

• Vetwrap, which is a stretchy bandaging tape that will not cling to feathers.

- Narrow masking tape or other paper tape.
- Scissors for clipping wings or cutting bandages. A small, sharp pair with 2- to 3-inch (5- to 7.5-cm) blades is the easiest to handle.
- Square-tipped tweezers.
- Needle-nosed pliers for pulling blood feathers.
- Locking forceps.
- Nail clippers for trimming nails. Good-quality cat claw scissors are excellent for small-to-medium parrots. Heavy-duty dog nail clippers work well for large macaws and cockatoos.
- Eyedropper or disposable pipettes.
- Syringes (without needles) in various sizes for administering oral medications or fluids.
- Curved, stainless-steel feeding (gavage) needles in sizes appropriate for the species you keep to administer fluids, medication, or food to weak or reluctant birds. Do not attempt to use these until your veterinarian has demonstrated the proper technique.
- Penlight.
- Heating pad.
- Self-activating warmers, which are inexpensive, nontoxic heating pads that produce heat through a safe chemical reaction when opened and exposed to air. These are commonly sold in sporting goods and camping stores as hand warmers. They are a fantastic, safe source of heat when electric heating pads cannot be used. I always carry some in my car for emergencies because I often transport young chicks. They are also a lifesaver during power failures if you have young chicks or sick birds that require heat.
- Styptic powder for stopping minor bleeding from toenails or the beak.
- Hydrogen peroxide solution for cleaning wounds.
- Povidone-iodine solution (Betadine) for treating minor wounds.
- Electrolyte solution (Pedialyte) for preventing and treating dehydration.
- Sterile saline solution for flushing out wounds or foreign bodies in the eye.
- Nontoxic, water-soluble white glue (Elmer's Glue-All) for repairing cracked eggs.
- Hobby drill. Although this item is not an absolute necessity, a small cordless hobby drill with an emery stone attachment works well for beak and nail grooming. Dremel brand tools are so popular among aviculturists and veterinarians that

Emergency Numbers

You should always keep a list of important phone numbers handy. These should include:
- Your regular avian veterinarian
- An after-hours emergency veterinary service
- A poison-control center
- Friends or acquaintances that might be able to assist you in any way during an emergency. I often receive phone calls from people who have been referred to me by local veterinarians, with questions about parrot breeding or behavioral issues.

their brand name is often incorrectly used as a verb, as in "Dremel the sharp points off the toenails." When using these for extended periods, be aware that they cause a heat buildup that can be uncomfortable for the birds. So stop often to allow the beak or nail to cool down.

You should keep these items together in an easily accessible container. One example is a plastic toolbox with a handle and removable trays, which keeps everything organized and easy to see. In a real emergency, even seconds count. You will also need a sturdy carrier to isolate the bird temporarily and to transport it to the veterinarian. If you have numerous parrots, you will want to keep a few of these on hand in case transporting more than one bird at a time is necessary.

To create a well-stocked emergency kit like the one described above, expect to spend between $75 and $175, depending on the quality and quantity of supplies. Of course, if it helps you save the life of even one beloved and expensive parrot, you will agree that it is a relative bargain.

Reference Materials

As knowledge of avian medicine, nutrition, and breeding grows, people learn new and better ways of caring for our feathered friends. One of the most valuable tools you can own is a good reference library. Keep current on new developments by subscribing to parrot magazines, attending conferences, and buying the latest books. Each bit of information that you pick up can help you in the quest to keep your birds healthy and productive.

As you have read in this chapter, keeping and breeding parrots is an expensive endeavor. The right tools, however, can save you plenty of time and heartache. In the end, I think you'll be glad that you (and your birds) got off to the right start.

Chapter Six

Adult Nutrition: The Foundation of Fertility

Nutritionally related illnesses are some of the most common problems seen in companion parrots today. Despite the wide array of formulated diets now on the market, many bird owners have yet to grasp the importance of proper avian nutrition. In pet birds, malnutrition tends to progress slowly and insidiously. The resultant illness often masks the underlying problem. Nature, however, is not so forgiving with breeding birds. A poorly nourished bird will be unable to breed or will produce weak, soft-shelled, or infertile eggs. The stress of breeding can even kill a nutritionally challenged bird.

The Essential Elements

Food is composed of four basic elements: proteins, carbohydrates, fats, and water. Proteins, carbohydrates, and fats supply energy. They also provide vitamins, minerals, and other trace elements necessary for life. Water cools the body, removes waste, and transports nutrients to the cells. The proper balance and quality of these elements will decide the difference between health and illness for your birds.

Proteins

Proteins, which are often referred to as the building blocks of life, are found throughout almost every part of the body, including bone, flesh, blood, organs, feathers, and beak. Proteins are also necessary for most of the body's chemical processes, such as healing and growth. All proteins are compounds made up from substances called amino acids. There are approximately 22 different amino acids that have been identified, and how they are combined determines the type of protein. Although some amino acids can be manufactured by the body, others must be derived from food. There are 10 that require a food source, and these are called *essential*. The essential amino acids are arginine, histidine, isoleucine, leucine, lysine, methionine, phenylalanine, threonine, tryptophan, and valine. A protein source that contains all 10 of these essentials is referred to as a *complete* protein and includes meat, milk, and eggs.

What then is the proper diet for a parrot? In truth, that question has no quick and easy answer. Many factors such as age, species, level of activity, and general health will dictate the proper diet *for that particular bird, at that particular point in its life.* Although there is such a thing as a general, all-purpose parrot diet, the aviculturist must adjust the nutritional levels as necessary to meet the needs of each individual. To do so, you'll need to understand some of the basics of nutrition.

Incomplete protein sources contain some or most of the essentials but not all. Creating a complete protein meal is possible by combining various foods with complementary amino acid levels. For example, most grains are deficient in lysine but contain sufficient methionine. Legumes (beans and peanuts) have enough lysine but lack methionine. By combining a grain with a legume, you will create a complete protein source. Two classic examples of this pairing are bean and rice dishes and the good old peanut butter sandwich.

Even complete proteins, however, will have little benefit if they are not bioavailable. This means that the body must be able to digest, absorb, and utilize the food properly. A high-protein diet that the bird cannot digest completely might provide less overall protein than a low-protein food that the bird digests and absorbs well. Manufacturers of well-formulated parrot diets usually use a combination of protein sources that are digestible and easily assimilated in the parrot gastrointestinal tract. This is one reason that birds on a high-quality formulated diet usually need to eat less than their counterparts who are fed a comparatively lower-quality (and less digestible) seed and grain mix.

If you assume that the protein content of a diet is complete and bioavailable, adult parrots do best on a maintenance level of about 12 to 16 percent protein, while growing chicks require between 19 to 22 percent. Adults that are sick, stressed, molting, or actively breeding might benefit from increased protein levels of up to 20 percent for a brief period. However, keeping them on high-protein diets for the long term is not advisable. Excess dietary protein is difficult to metabolize and can seriously exacerbate underlying kidney and liver problems.

Carbohydrates

Whereas proteins can be thought of as the structure of a body, carbohydrates are the fuel that drives it. Carbohydrates supply energy and heat, and they support the metabolic processes necessary for life. Carbohydrates are derived mainly from plants. They are composed of starches (digestible polysaccharides), sugars (monosaccharides and disaccharides), and fiber, which is indigestible or *resistant* carbohydrate.

Most carbohydrates are converted by the body into glucose, a simple sugar that is carried through the bloodstream to supply cells with energy. Excess glucose goes to the liver. There it is turned into glycogen and stored in the liver and muscles as a ready fuel source. Once the liver and muscles are fully stocked, any remaining glucose is turned into fat for long-term storage. Because virtually all diets contain carbohydrates, there is really no such thing as a carbohydrate deficiency. Short-term deprivation, such as in a bird that has been fasted, can cause low blood sugar levels, which is known as *hypoglycemia*. This condition is usually transient, however, and will likely resolve as soon as the bird is fed. Excess carbohydrates lead to weight gain and obesity, which can contribute to heart and lung problems, diabetes, liver and kidney disease, and skeletal problems.

Because carbohydrates primarily supply energy, there is no average requirement. The amount your birds need will depend on their age, species, level of activity, and the temperature at which they are maintained. If you notice signs of obesity, cut back on the amount of food or increase the activity level by adding toys or increasing the cage size. Obesity is much less common in birds being fed a high-quality formulated diet than it is in birds on a seed-based regime.

Fats

While dietary fats often have a negative connotation these days, a certain amount of fats is vital to sustain life. Fats (also correctly called *lipids*) are a concentrated source of stored energy, aid in the absorption of some vitamins, act as precursors for several hormonelike substances, serve as insulation for the body, and give foods a pleasant "mouth-feel." Lipids are composed primarily of three types of fatty acids: saturated, monounsaturated, and polyunsaturated. Saturated fats come mostly from animal sources, such as meat and dairy products, although coconut and palm oils are also highly saturated. This fat is usually solid at room temperature. A dietary excess of this type of fat is associated with cardiovascular and other degenerative diseases.

A carefully balanced diet contributes to growth, feather development, fertility, and overall health.

A caged bird cannot choose its own diet like its wild counterpart could.

Unsaturated fats come primarily from plants and fish. These should make up a majority of the fat in your bird's diet. These are usually liquid at room temperature. Polyunsaturated fats include sunflower, safflower, sesame, corn, and soy oils. Monounsaturated fats include olive, peanut, avocado, and canola (rapeseed) oils. In moderation, these healthy lipids supply the necessary essential fatty acids and help to make the diet palatable.

In general, fat levels of 4 to 7 percent are suitable for adult parrot maintenance and 8 to 15 percent for growing chicks, depending on the species. Adult Amazons and other sedentary species might require lower fat levels, perhaps 3 percent. On the other hand, adult macaws often do better on a higher fat intake, usually between 8 to 12 percent. The same is true for babies. Amazon chicks should be fed a lower-fat, hand-feeding formula with 8 to 9 percent fat, whereas macaw chicks need 12 to 15 percent fat to grow properly without stunting. Please note that these levels are not absolutes. Many in the world of avian nutrition still disagree about what constitutes a proper diet for parrots. However, the ranges I've given encompass most of the formulated diets on the market and express the majority opinion.

Water

Although it is not often thought of as a nutrient, water is essential for all bodily functions. Water cools the body, transports nutrients to cells, removes waste products, and serves as a medium for chemical reactions. A deficiency of water is called dehydration and will lead to death if not corrected promptly. The amount of water that a bird needs will vary according to species, type of diet, and many other factors. Budgies and zebra finches seem to metabolize water from food sources and drink comparatively little. Most other species depend on a regular source of fresh water, however, and will die if deprived of it for more than a day or two. Keep in mind that birds fed a dry-seed or pelleted diet will require more water than those fed a diet high in juicy fruits and vegetables. No matter what the diet or what species you are dealing with, be certain that a supply of clean, fresh water is available at all times.

Vitamins

Vitamins are organic substances that regulate cellular functions. Although most vitamins are derived from food, certain ones can be manufactured in the body. Vitamins are divided into two groups, fat soluble and water soluble. Fat-soluble vitamins, which include A, D, E, and K, are stored in the body, primarily in the liver and body fats. Water-soluble vitamins, which include all B-complex vitamins and C, remain in body tissues for a relatively short time, so they must be replenished on a constant basis. Because fat-soluble vitamins are stored, building up toxic amounts is possible if these are oversupplemented. The greatest danger lies with A and D_3 in birds, whereas E and K are less likely to cause problems. Water-soluble vitamins are rarely toxic, except in extreme cases of overdose. Nevertheless, do not add supplemental vitamins if your birds are on a good-quality formulated diet, which should supply all the nutrients they need. If they are not yet eating a proper diet, then add a vitamin supplement. However, follow the label directions, and do not overdose.

Minerals

Minerals are inorganic substances contained in the earth's crust. Small amounts of these substances are taken up by plants and animals and become part of the food chain. Minerals play a critical role in the body and are essential for life. A few, like calcium and phosphorus, are required in significant amounts and are sometimes referred to as *macrominerals.* Others are needed in only very minute amounts and are known as *microminerals* or *trace* minerals. Roughly 12 minerals have been identified as essential for a healthy avian diet, and recommended dietary minimums have been set. Several other minerals, however, are less clearly understood but appear to be important nonetheless.

Putting It All Together

You might feel overwhelmed at the prospect of planning a suitable diet. Not only must all the nutrients be available, but they must also be available in correct ratios so that they do not create imbalances in the others. Because the birds cannot fly around and choose from an unlimited supply of food, they depend on what you put into the dish. So what do you put into the dish?

Seed Diets

By now you have probably come to realize that a seed-only diet is insufficient and downright neglectful. Adding a few fruits and vegetables is an improvement but will still not cover all the nutritional bases, especially for breeding birds and their fast-growing offspring. For example, seeds, fruits, and many vegetables are notoriously low in calcium, so a bird on such a diet is almost guaranteed a calcium deficiency (hypocalcemia) unless supplemental calcium is added. To make matters worse, fatty acids, phytates, and oxalates present in seeds, grains, and some vegetables bind with calcium and further inhibit its absorption.

Calcium also works synergistically with phosphorus. The two must be available in proper ratios for optimal function. In parrots, that ratio is approximately 2:1 (two parts calcium per one part phosphorus) for maintenance and perhaps slightly higher during active egg laying. Many of the commonly fed items in a bird's diet are high in phosphorus and low or absent in calcium, including sunflower seeds, safflower seeds, peanuts, corn, apples, and grapes. Sunflower seeds, for example, have approximately seven parts phosphorus to one part calcium, and safflower seeds and peanuts are not much better.

I frequently run into old-time breeders who insist that they've used a seed-based diet for years and years and their birds are doing just fine, thank you. Of course, they had that hen that died from egg binding, and the babies with splayed legs, and the 15-year-old Amazon with arthritis and liver troubles, and the cockatoo that died from a heart attack, and so on. These people don't seem to understand that these are largely *nutritional* diseases. Most

medium-to-large parrots should live well into their forties or fifties or beyond without any significant degenerative diseases. A seed-based diet usually will not kill a parrot quickly, but you can be certain that this diet will kill it slowly and insidiously.

Besides the above-mentioned problem with calcium and phosphorus, seed diets are also deficient in vitamins A, D_3, E, K, several of the B-complex vitamins, certain amino acids, and several trace elements. They are extremely high in fat and can negatively affect the absorption of some nutrients. By adding a carefully chosen mix of fruits, vegetables, grains, dairy products, and vitamin and mineral supplements, you might be able to offer your birds a fair diet, provided, of course, that they eat everything in the mix completely. In reality, birds will choose their favorite items, and the diet becomes imbalanced and inadequate.

Formulated (Pelleted) Diets

A simple answer exists—to offer your birds a formulated diet. These diets were developed after years of research about avian nutrition. Formulated parrot diets come in two forms, pelleted and extruded, although most people in the avian community use the term *pellets* to refer to both types. In general, true pellets consist of a mixture of coarsely ground grains and other food products, supplemented with vitamins and minerals, and pressed into hard, cylindrical pieces. These diets tend to be tan or light brown in color and have a natural grain aroma.

Extruded diets begin with much the same ingredients, which are then finely ground, cooked to enhance digestibility, and forced through a die and shaped in a process called extrusion. Extruded brands often contain flavorings and colorings. They are available in a wide variety of shapes, colors, and sizes. For the sake of simplicity, the term *pellets* will be used to refer to both types of formulated foods even though extruded diets are more common these days. Both of these diets are based on the same concept as dry dog and cat foods, which is to provide complete and balanced nutrition in each bite.

Detractors offer three main arguments against feeding pellets. First, they claim that no such thing as a complete diet exists since no one yet fully understands parrot nutrition. Although this is true, the same argument can be applied toward any diet. Your birds will certainly have a much better chance at total nutrition with a formulated diet than they will with the "throw-it-in-the-bowl-and-see-what-they-like" school of nutrition. Over the years, pellet manufacturers have tweaked and fiddled with the diets constantly as research suggests methods for improvement.

The second argument waged against pellets is that they are unnatural. Actually, most of the ingredients found in pellets are natural food items for parrots, albeit in a processed form. Today's common seed mixes, on the other hand, tend to use a number of seeds and grains that are not normally found in the range countries of most parrots. More importantly, people need to get over the romanticized belief that they should replicate the natural diet of birds in the wild. Most parrots in the wild are opportunistic feeders and will consume just about anything to meet their caloric needs, including insects, lizards, and carrion. Wild parrots likely do not reach their maximum possible life span due, in part, to the difficulty of obtaining sufficient and varied nutrients. Captive diets can and should be an improvement over free-ranging diets, not a duplication of them.

The final argument against pellets is that they're boring and fail to offer taste and tactile stimulation to the bird. This smacks of anthropomorphism. (Because pellets look boring to people, people assume they are boring to birds.) This argument has several problems. First of all, parrots are creatures of habit and will often choose to eat one food to the near exclusion of others. Therefore, lack of choice does not necessarily imply boredom. Secondly, parrots do not have the same sense of taste that humans possess, so gauging taste preferences is very difficult. Although birds might show strong preferences for one food over another, these preferences could be due to familiarity, taste, color, shape, size, or many other factors.

For example, I have a wild-caught Moluccan cockatoo that came to me on an exclusive diet of black-striped sunflower seeds. Because that was all he would eat, that became the only food item that his previous owners offered him. He was in poor health and terrible feathering, yet he stubbornly refused any other foods. After months of experimenting with different formulated diets, I finally found one he would accept. Now, 15 years later, Mikey is healthy and beautiful. He's still food obsessed, but now he's obsessed with pellets

Offer your birds a variety of formulated foods, fruits, vegetables, grains, and nuts.

and will not touch seeds. He has expanded his palate to include many different brands of pellets but shows a definite preference for formulated diets over any fresh foods.

Maintenance Diets

Although most avian researchers, veterinarians, and nutritionists seem to concur that a formulated diet is essential for long life and optimal health, it need not be the only food your birds eat. Between 20 to 30 percent of the diet can be made up of fresh fruits, vegetables, seeds, nuts, grains, and people food. Keep in mind, however, that this means that roughly 70 to 80 percent of the bird's intake must be the formulated diet. Some well-meaning people claim that they are feeding a pelleted diet. However, what they actually do is fill a crock in the parrot's cage with pellets, then spend the rest of the day stuffing the bird with assorted treats while the pellets sit uneaten. I usually feed an assortment of pellets free choice (available at all times) and offer small amounts of fruits, vegetables, or other treats as a snack late in the morning.

You can adapt this basic diet to meet the special needs of any species you keep. Because macaws require relatively high levels of fat, I offer my macaws a small dish of mixed in-shell nuts every day along with their other treats. A few species (Eclectus, hanging parrots, and fig parrots, for example) seem to do best on a diet that's roughly 60 percent pellets and 40 percent high-vitamin fruits and vegetables. Lories and lorikeets need an even higher percentage of fruits. However, they still do best with a formulated lory powder as a base diet to provide the proteins, fats, and vitamins they require. For most parrot species, researchers recommend protein levels between 12 to 16 percent and fat levels between 4 to 7 percent for a maintenance diet.

Breeding Diets

You should consider several factors when changing a bird's diet during breeding season. A good breeding diet should
• Act as a psychological stimulus to induce pairs to nest
• Increase the hen's level of nutrition to provide the extra nutrients required for egg production and embryonic survival
• Provide a healthy growth diet for parent-fed chicks

Although pairs might produce successfully on standard maintenance fare, it will often be at the female's expense as she depletes her body stores to create eggs. On the other hand, feeding a breeding diet year-round is just as dangerous, because the higher levels of fats and proteins will likely cause obesity and a host of other medical problems in nonproducing birds. Ironically, one of the major problems associated with the overuse of breeding diets is infertility in males, due primarily to obesity.

Many aviculturists have had success in inducing breeding activity by sharply increasing the amount of soft food (fruits and vegetables) offered at the beginning of the season. Parrot species that are traditionally spring breeders often respond to seasonal cues, such as increased day length, higher humidity and barometric pressure, and an increase in the supply of fresh food. This tactic is somewhat less effective with species like African greys, which tend to breed during the dry season in the wild and are often winter breeders in captivity. The other problem with this method arises when the fruit and vegetable portion of the diet exceeds 30 percent or so of the food intake. In this case, it becomes counterproductive since the hen is not likely consuming enough fats and proteins to sustain her during egg production.

The problem can be tackled in a few ways. To begin with, you should switch to a breeding pellet as the season approaches. These are usually between 18 to 22 percent protein and 7 to 10 percent fat. They will contain higher levels of calcium and other nutrients to support reproduction and growth. If you want to increase the soft-food portion of the diet beyond 30 percent, you can incorporate the pellets into the soft food. During breeding season, I make up a birdie casserole that includes cooked whole-wheat pasta, brown rice, beans, chopped sweet potatoes, chopped kale or spinach, wheat germ, crumbled breeding pellets, and anything else I feel like tossing in. The birds love it, and it

Actively breeding birds require a diet higher in fats, proteins, and calcium.

chicks, or they might stuff the chicks with relatively low-nutrient foods instead of the highly nutritional pellets. I once gave my macaws an ear of corn a few days after a baby hatched. When I peeked into the nest box later, I saw that the chick's crop was completely packed full with nothing but kernels of corn. Although a few feedings like this won't hurt a healthy baby, selective food choices of this sort will not provide the range of nutrients required for growth. If you make sure that the parents are eating mostly pellets and other highly nutritious foods, you'll be reasonably certain that the chicks are receiving proper nutrition. As always, provide plenty of clean, fresh water. You'll find that the parents require a greatly increased water and food intake while feeding babies, so keep those dishes full!

Post Breeding

Once breeding season is over, the time has come to make the transition back to a maintenance diet. Continue to feed breeder pellets for a week or two after removing the chicks to allow the parents to build up their nutritional reserves. Then make the switch back to maintenance formulas. Start to dry out the diet slightly by reducing the amount of soft food. For pairs without a clearly defined breeding season, you can simply cycle the diet from maintenance to breeding and back again once or twice a year, adjusting as necessary when they show signs of reproductive activity.

allows me to increase the amount of soft food without reducing their overall pellet intake. They get a dish of this mixture each morning in addition to the dry breeding pellets. When feeding any soft foods, however, always remove the uneaten portion after three or four hours since these are an incredible growth medium for bacteria and fungi.

The breeding diet described above will provide a solid foundation to carry the parents through breeding, egg laying, and chick rearing. Be sure you do not offer too many individual fruits and vegetables to the parents while they're feeding

Food Storage and Safety

No matter what you are feeding, you must be sure that the food is fresh, is unspoiled, and contains viable nutrients. Most pelleted diets have an expiration date, or a date of manufacture, stamped right onto the bag. A few companies code these dates, so ask your supplier or call the manufacturer if you are uncertain. In general, formulated diets that contain preservatives (natural or artificial) are considered fresh for about a year after manufacture, assuming they're stored under cool, dry conditions. Extreme heat and humidity will shorten the shelf life, but refrigeration or freezing will extend it.

Preservative-free brands have a shorter shelf life and should probably be refrigerated after opening.

Seed mixes are not normally dated, so gauging the freshness is difficult. Most seed crops are harvested just once or maybe twice a year and kept in storage. If you purchase seed mixes, buy only from a reputable manufacturer and buy only from suppliers who have a rapid turnover of product. Otherwise, you might be getting food that has been sitting in storage for a year or more. Some books recommend sprouting a few seeds to test for freshness, but many of the mixes are treated and processed in ways that will hamper germination, even if the seeds are relatively fresh.

Poison Alert

Always store seeds and grains in cool, dry, airtight containers. Exposure to heat and air will cause the oils to turn rancid and encourage the growth of molds and fungi. Most of these are invisible, but they form dangerous compounds known as mycotoxins. You cannot normally see, smell, or taste mycotoxins, but they are deadly poisons. Depending on the type and the amount present, effects range from low-level chronic damage to the liver, kidneys, and immune system to sudden toxicity and death over just a few days.

Aflatoxin, a mycotoxin common to peanuts and corn, is a potent cancer-causing agent that attacks the kidneys and liver. The USDA inspects peanuts destined for human consumption to ensure aflatoxin levels fall below federal limits, but improper storage at a later date might cause fungal growth. I feed only human-grade peanuts to my birds, and I limit them to just a few each week.

The important points to remember here are that you should buy only the freshest food possible, store it properly, and immediately discard any food that looks moldy or discolored or that smells rancid or musty. Keep in mind that replacing a bag of questionable food is much cheaper than replacing a beloved and valuable parrot that dies from mycotoxin exposure.

Chapter Seven

Flock Health: When You Become the HMO

Flock medicine is not just single bird medicine multiplied *x* times. In an aviary, the flock becomes an entity unto itself. The health of the flock can be no better than the health of any individual. In other words, one sick bird can seriously endanger all the rest. For this reason, disease prevention and detection are critically important to prevent outbreaks that could spread throughout your collection.

Choosing an Avian Veterinarian

The first step in any health plan is to choose a doctor, and birds are no different. Don't assume that you can use the same veterinarian who treats your dog or cat. Parrots are a completely different specialty. Even the most highly qualified dog veterinarian might be lost when it comes to birds.

Do not wait until you have a sick bird to begin your search for a qualified avian veterinarian. You'll want to find the right person, develop a rapport, and plan out a health care strategy in advance. You don't want to be struggling to communicate with a stranger while your birds are dropping off their perches from some mystery illness. Before you choose a practitioner, you need to ask several questions and settle several issues. Your relationship with your veterinarian should be a partnership. Like any good partnership, you both need to know what to expect from the other. Some pertinent questions include the following.

• How many birds do you see in a week? (This indicates the level of experience and comfort with avian patients.)

• Are you comfortable with avian pediatrics? (Some otherwise great veterinarians see lots of adult pet birds but rarely encounter young chicks.)

• Do you breed birds yourself?

• Who handles your clients when you're unavailable? (Is this person as qualified?)

• Are you on call for after-hours emergencies? If not, where do you refer emergencies?

• Are you willing to visit my aviary on a periodic schedule to perform routine flock diagnostics and review husbandry?

• What is your fee schedule? Do you have a breeder program? Will you accept a payment plan if an emergency arises that is beyond my financial resources at that moment?

• What diagnostics do you feel are important for a new bird exam?

A good veterinarian will likely have some questions to ask you in return, although he or she might be hesitant to voice them. You can build trust by addressing some of these issues up front and making it clear you are open to discuss any questions that might arise. For example, are you willing to put up the money for diagnostic tests that the doctor feels are necessary? Nothing frustrates a good practitioner more than having to play guessing games over a sick bird because the owner refuses to pay for needed tests. The same goes for new bird exams. If you are trying to cut corners and your veterinarian is trying to ensure the health and safety of your other birds by screening out disease carriers, you will likely be at odds. Will you keep appointments and honor the schedule? Veterinarians, like any health care provider, are extremely busy professionals. Missing or showing up late for appointments, frequently rescheduling at the last minute, and abusing the privilege of phone consultations will not endear you to the doctor or clinic staff.

Do you create emergencies? A broken wing is an emergency. A bird that has steadily deteriorated over

Avian Professionals

To find an avian specialist, ask other folks in your local bird community for a referral or call the Association of Avian Veterinarians (AAV) for a listing of members in your area. AAV is a professional group that keeps its members informed of the latest developments in avian medicine, promotes research, and provides education and support to the avian community. You can reach them at (561) 393-8901 or visit their Web site at *www.aav.org* to find a listing by state.

the course of a week from an infection that you chose to ignore is abuse and should not have progressed to the emergency stage. A dear friend of mine who is a dedicated avian veterinarian says she often receives emergency calls in the wee hours of the night from frantic owners who say that their pet is on the cage floor, barely breathing. When she asks how long the symptoms have been present, they will blithely respond that the bird has "looked funny" for several days. Unfortunately, by the time she receives the call, it is often too late. Birds are masters at hiding signs of disease. By the time a parrot looks sick, it is likely to be critically ill. If you respond promptly and appropriately to any early-warning signs of disease, you will have far fewer emergencies and much greater success in keeping your flock alive and well.

After you have discussed all these issues with your new veterinarian, you have probably formed the basis for a trusting and mutually enjoyable working relationship. If, for any reason, you do not feel comfortable, do not hesitate to continue your search for a different practitioner. Once you have found the right person, the time has come to begin your health plan.

Quarantine

The first place to start is with quarantine procedures. Any new birds you bring in should be placed into strict quarantine for a minimum of 60 days. Because many viruses have extremely long incubation periods or can exist in a carrier state, this will not protect your flock from all disease introductions. However, it is a good start. For quarantine to be effective, the quarantined birds must be totally isolated from the aviary. This means no transfer of equipment, no back and forth movement of people or pets, and no shared airflow. For outside aviaries, a separate building located away from the others and serviced last is the best method.

Once you enter the quarantine building, you should consider yourself potentially contaminated. Do not reenter your normal aviaries or go near pet birds until you have showered and changed clothes. Disease is transmitted in three primary ways: through direct contact (bird to bird), through the air, or through fomite

transmission. Fomite transmission is a fancy way of saying that germs transfer between hosts by latching onto an object or person and hitching a ride. You can transfer germs on your hands, clothing, hair, or shoes. Rodents, insects, and other critters can act as fomites in spreading infections. By using the same broom to sweep quarantine and regular buildings, the broom becomes a fomite capable of carrying disease. Always keep separate equipment and food supplies for your quarantine area, and thoroughly disinfect anything that leaves the building.

Of course, if you're breeding birds in your home and do not have a separate building available, then the issue of quarantine becomes a bit stickier. You can use a spare room. Keep in mind, though, that you (and anyone else in your household) will be potentially contaminated once you enter the room. I have a spare room with an outdoor entrance and use that for quarantine. The biggest problem with in-house quarantine is airflow. If you have forced-air heating and cooling, then any diseases will be quickly spread throughout the entire house unless you can somehow seal off the room or provide adequate filtration. I'm lucky to have radiant heat, which doesn't create airflow patterns to the same degree. I keep a good-quality air filter running in the quarantine area at all times and have an ionizer in the hallway that separates that room from the rest of the house. Ionizers put a mild electric charge into the air, which prevents dust and other particle matter from remaining suspended in the air and being carried about. The particles drop to the floor or cling to walls, which can be sprayed with a disinfectant solution and wiped or mopped. This certainly isn't a foolproof method, but it will offer some degree of protection. Keep in mind that air purifiers work by drawing air through them, so they will create airflow patterns of their own. Locate purifiers so contaminated air is pulled away from, not drawn toward, your healthy birds.

New Bird Exams

Now that you've established quarantine procedures, your next step is to begin new bird exams. Whenever possible, I like to bring newly purchased birds directly to my veterinarian's office. This avoids the stress of bringing them home, settling them into quarantine, then catching them and stuffing them into a carrier for a trip to the veterinarian a few days later. On the other hand, some veterinarians feel that it's a good idea to intentionally allow the birds to be stressed by moving them two or three days before the exam, so that any subclinical disease breaks (becomes apparent) due to the stress. Ask your veterinarian which way he or she prefers to handle this issue. The bird clinic I use has a drop-off service, which allows me to bring in birds without an appointment, leave them to be

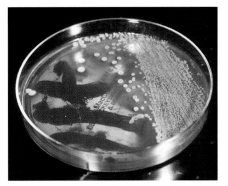

A culture plate (MacConkey agar) displays heavy bacterial growth.

examined at the doctor's convenience, and pick them up later. We agree in advance what tests should be run. If extra tests are indicated, the office calls to discuss it.

The minimum that a new bird visit should include is a thorough physical exam, weight evaluation, fecal Gram's stain, and a complete blood count (CBC). Ideally, all birds should be tested for chlamydia (psittacosis), polyomavirus, and PBFD (psittacine beak and feather disease). At the very least, test susceptible species or individuals with likely exposure. The addition of a blood chemistry panel, bacterial cultures, and radiographs will give you the most accurate picture possible about the health of your new acquisition. If the bird was previously maintained outdoors, then fecal smears and flotation are important to detect the presence of intestinal parasites.

Physical Exam

A good physical exam should start with quietly observing the bird

Forehead
Eye
Cere
Nares
Lores
Upper Mandible
Lower Mandible
Throat
Breast
Abdomen
Thigh
Foot
Toe

Crown
Eye Ring
Ear Coverts
Nape
Wing
Rump
Vent
(Cloaca)
Hock

A thorough physical exam should look at the bird from head to toe.

while it sits in its carrier or on a perch. Labored breathing, lameness, difficulty in perching, and abnormal behavior all indicate possible illness. A healthy parrot will appear alert and should have bright eyes and shiny feathers. After a brief observation, the next step would be a hands-on exam that looks at the eyes, ears, nose, mouth, and vent (cloaca) for signs of swelling, discharge, inflammation, or infection. The veterinarian should listen to the heart and respiratory system with a stethoscope to detect any abnormal sounds, and gently tug on or bend the wings and legs to check for signs of discomfort. He or she should gently evert the bird's cloacal tissue with a moistened cotton swab to check for evidence of papillomas. These wart-like growths can appear throughout the body in infected birds, but are commonly found inside the cloaca. Finally, the bird should be weighed and compared to normal weight ranges for its species. Since weight loss is often the first sign of disease, this is a valuable indicator of overall health. This will also help determine if a bird is significantly overweight and requires dietary controls.

Diagnostic Tests

During the physical exam, your veterinarian can draw blood and swab fluids for a wide variety of diagnostic tests. A description of individual tests and the diseases they detect follows.

Gram's stains are used to determine the type and quantity of bacteria and yeast in a bird's system. A swab of body fluid is collected, usually from the mouth or vent. This fluid is smeared onto a microscope slide and treated with special dyes. Gram-positive bacteria, which usually do not cause disease in birds, will appear dark blue or violet after being exposed to the dyes. Gram-negative bacteria appear as light red or pink and are not considered normal flora in birds. Significant numbers of Gram-negative bacteria indicates an infection, which should be treated with antibiotics. If a bird shows relatively small numbers of Gram-negative bacteria and appears healthy, most veterinarians today feel that treatment is not required.

Cultures and sensitivities: A culture can be performed in addition to a Gram's stain or instead of it. In a culture, a sterile swab is used to collect fluid from the site of the suspected infection. This could include pus from a wound or drainage from sinuses. In a bird without obvious signs of infection, a bit of fecal material is usually used. This material is then streaked across a culture plate, which is a shallow dish filled with substances that encourage bacterial or fungal growth. The plate is placed into an incubator and allowed to grow for 24 hours. If bacterial growth is not evident, the material may be transferred to a culture plate containing a different growth medium and incubated for another 24-hour period.

If a bacterium does grow, it can be identified and tested for sensitivity to different antibiotics. In the sensitivity test, small paper disks treated with various antibiotics are placed on top of the growing bacteria. By watching to see which disk

Normal healthy cloacal tissue has a smooth appearance.

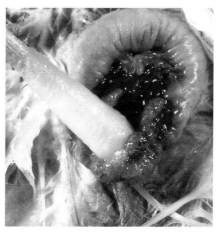

Papillomas are evidenced by bumpy red cloacal tissue that resembles a raspberry.

kills the most bacteria, the veterinarian will know which antibiotic is most likely to clear up the infection successfully.

A complete blood count (CBC) is a common test that uses a small amount of blood, usually drawn from a clipped toenail or sometimes from a vein in the leg, neck, or wing. This test gives a wealth of information about the bird's health. It examines different components of the blood, including red blood cells (which carry oxygen), white blood cells (which fight infection), thrombocytes (which are required for clotting), serum protein, plasma, and other elements.

A blood chemistry panel is a more detailed blood test that examines the blood serum for a wide variety of chemical indicators. Any of these indicators that fall outside of established ranges can indicate

disease, malnutrition, or decreased organ function. This test is a wonderful evaluation of the bird's overall health and nutritional level. I have chemistry panels done on each of my pet birds every few years, and I periodically do random sampling of my aviary to detect any latent disease or nutritional problems that might be brewing unnoticed.

Chlamydia testing: Chlamydiosis (most commonly called psittacosis, but also known as ornithosis or parrot fever) is a highly contagious disease caused by a bacterium called *Chlamydia psittaci.* It is a zoonotic disease, which means it can be passed from birds to humans. It is also a reportable disease, so most state health departments require notification of outbreaks. If an outbreak occurs in a pet shop or aviary, health officials will enforce a strict quarantine and treatment protocol. Symptoms of chlamydiosis in birds can vary from listlessness, loss of appetite, yellow or lime green urates, and nasal discharge to sudden death without any preceding symptoms. Some birds, especially cockatiels, will carry the disease and spread it to others without ever showing signs of clinical illness.

Although the disease does not commonly spread to healthy humans, the elderly or immunosuppressed are at risk. In humans, it causes flulike symptoms that are often mild, but can turn into serious or life-threatening pneumonia if not diagnosed properly and treated with the appropriate antibiotics. If you or a family member

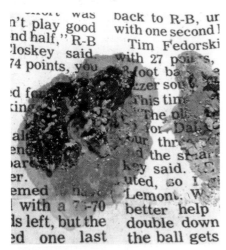

Bright green urates indicate chlamydiosis or other diseases which affect the liver.

experience flu symptoms that do not abate after a normal time, you should mention to your doctor that you have birds. Of course, use common sense. I once casually mentioned to my former doctor that I bred parrots. He had recently seen a scary article about psittacosis. From that moment forward, he tried to prescribe doxycycline (the drug of choice for chlamydia) every time I sneezed or stubbed my toe. I could not seem to make him understand that my flock had been tested and showed no signs of chlamydia, so I eventually changed doctors.

Several different methods can be used to test birds for chlamydia. Some recent research studies on chlamydia detection were performed at Texas A&M University. They recommended using a combination of two tests known as PCR (polymerase chain reaction) and EBA (elementary body agglutination assay) to achieve the most accurate diagnosis. Your veterinarian will determine which test (or tests) to implement. Infected birds are isolated, given supportive care, and treated with doxycycline for a period of 45 to 60 days. Doxycycline is available in several forms and can be administered orally, by injection, or via medicated food. In the past, treating the entire flock each year prior to breeding season with chlortetracycline-laced feeds was common practice, even if the birds showed no evidence of infection. Most veterinarians now advise against this practice because it only

encourages the growth of antibiotic-resistant strains. New and easier methods of treatment are currently being investigated, including the use of the antibiotic enrofloxacin in the drinking water.

Fecal Tests

Fecal analysis is a microscopic evaluation of the bird's droppings to detect intestinal parasites. Certain parasites, especially *Giardia*, can be difficult to detect, and the stool sample must be very fresh (less than 15 minutes old). It is a good idea to run fecal tests on any birds that have been kept outdoors, especially in warmer climates, or if they have had access to the ground where these parasites can frequently be found.

DNA Probes

DNA probes are highly sensitive and specific tests that allow certain pathogens to be identified in a blood or cell sample. At present, DNA probes are available for two major avian viruses, polyomavirus and psittacine beak and feather disease (PBFD).

Polyomavirus is a highly fatal viral disease that usually attacks unweaned parrot chicks. The first strain identified causes budgerigar fledgling disease, which causes high mortality and feather abnormalities in baby budgies. Another form of the virus attacks mostly larger parrots and is commonly referred to as polyoma or polyomavirus. Polyoma usually attacks without warning. The first sign is often sudden death in chicks. Symptoms that may appear include depression, loss of appetite, subcutaneous hemorrhages (bleeding under the skin), vomiting, and delayed crop emptying. Infected chicks usually die within 24 to 48 hours after exhibiting symptoms. Any that do survive may become carriers of the disease and shed the virus to others. Adult birds rarely become seriously ill or show signs of the disease, although they can be infected and become carriers. Adult birds apparently eventually clear the virus from their system and stop shedding, although they can become reinfected from exposure to other infected birds and start the cycle all over again. Budgies, however, appear to remain carriers and shed the virus throughout their lives, so be cautious about keeping budgies if you also keep larger parrots.

By testing your existing flock, you will know if any adults show signs of polyomavirus infection and possible carrier state. Because carriers can shed the virus intermittently, testing birds twice in a year (before and after breeding season) might be necessary to catch transient disease. The DNA probe test commonly used is simple and requires only a swab of the bird's cloaca. If none of your birds test positive for the disease and you routinely test new birds with a comprehensive polyoma panel before adding them to the aviary, then you will be relatively safe from polyoma outbreaks. If you do find that you have likely carriers, your choice is to cull (remove) those birds

from your collection and retest the others periodically or vaccinate the flock and any babies they produce.

A bitter debate is currently occurring among veterinarians and researchers about the need for vaccination. Since it is primarily a neonatal (baby) disease, many feel that vaccinating adults is not necessary, provided tests show that the flock is not carrying infection and no untested birds are added to the collection. They further believe that vaccinating chicks is unnecessary if the breeder keeps them until they are fully weaned and past the danger stage, provided they are not exposed to chicks from other aviaries or pet shops, which might have carriers. The other group believes that all birds, regardless of age, should be vaccinated as a preventative measure. Both groups, however, agree that unweaned chicks should be vaccinated if they are being sold or otherwise exposed to other people's birds before they are fully weaned. That includes bringing your chicks to a bird fair or club meeting, taking a trip to the veterinarian's office, or bringing an untested bird into the house. As a general rule, once a chick leaves your premises, it is potentially infected and should be vaccinated and kept separately from any other chicks in the house.

In my aviary, I have never had a positive polyoma test result, and I do not sell unweaned babies. Therefore, I have chosen not to vaccinate routinely. I will, however, vaccinate chicks before they leave the nursery if their new owners request it, and I would certainly vaccinate any unweaned chicks I transfer for any reason. My veterinarian agrees with the decision and was, in fact, instrumental in helping me decide. The main problem with the vaccine is that it is still very expensive and requires a series of two injections, then yearly boosters. At the current price, it would cost me approximately $3,000 a year to vaccinate all adults and chicks. I would gladly spend the money if I believed my birds were at risk. However, my veterinarian believes that it is unnecessary, and the disruption and stress of routinely catching and injecting adult breeders every year might offset any potential benefit. Again, this is a volatile issue in the avian medical community. Discuss it with your veterinarian and try to arrive at a decision you are both comfortable with.

PBFD, or psittacine beak and feather disease, is a highly contagious fatal virus that can affect almost any species of parrot, although it is most common in Old World psittacines, including cockatoos, African greys, Eclectus, and lovebirds. It usually strikes birds under the age of three years, but occasionally older birds show signs of infection. There are two forms of PBFD, chronic and acute. The acute form, which is most common in young chicks, often begins with depression, crop stasis, and deformities and lesions in emerging feathers. It usually results in death within a few days to a few weeks.

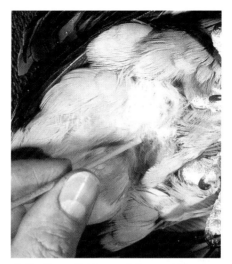

Collecting a fluid sample by swabbing the cloaca.

In chicks that survive the acute phase, or in those that are infected at a later age, the disease usually presents in a chronic form. In the chronic form, there is a symmetric and progressive emergence of abnormal feathers. Feathers may appear clubbed, curled, or show evidence of hemorrhaging inside the feather shaft. In some cases, beak deformities and necrosis may appear. The chronic form is also fatal, although some individuals can live for many years before succumbing, usually to secondary infections. In a few reported cases, New World parrots (macaws and Pionus) have appeared to recover completely from PBFD. However, for most species showing clinical signs, survival is unlikely.

Because many diseases and behaviors can affect feather forma-

Birds suffering from PBFD will show feather loss, feather deformities, and possibly overgrown or damaged beaks.

tion, getting a definitive diagnosis is important. A DNA probe of a blood sample will confirm the presence of the virus. PBFD is much less common now than it was during the heyday of importation, but it is still out there. You cannot get too complacent. Your veterinarian might recommend that you test all your birds and any new additions, especially susceptible species. Due to the contagious nature of this virus, any birds testing positive must be removed from the premises or you run a high risk of spreading the disease throughout your flock. Euthanizing infected individuals is not always necessary, although those in advanced stages might be experiencing pain and suffering. You might be able to place an infected yet reasonably healthy bird into a pet home, provided it is the only bird in the household. Of course, the pet owners must understand the disease is contagious, progressive, and usually fatal, and they should not introduce other birds into the home or visit bird fairs and aviaries because of the risk of transporting the virus on their clothes and hair. With proper care, good nutrition, and a stress-free environment, a parrot with chronic PBFD can survive in reasonable health for many years. It might be someone's cherished pet during those years.

There is currently an experimental vaccine for PBFD, but it is not commercially available. With simple DNA probe testing, however, identifying and removing infected individuals should be possible, thus eliminating PBFD from aviaries.

Pacheco's disease virus (PDV) is caused by an avian herpesvirus and usually causes severe or fatal liver disease. Numerous strains of PDV exist, with a wide variation in fatality. Some strains kill over 80 percent of exposed parrots, yet others will cause just a few deaths and scattered illness. Symptoms include sudden death, depression, diarrhea (which might contain blood), green or yellow urates, and tremors or seizures. Pacheco's can appear suddenly in a flock and then disappear just as quickly. Because most infected birds die or develop symptoms within three to ten days of being exposed to the virus, an outbreak might be considered over if two or three weeks pass with no further signs of death or illness.

Unfortunately, birds that recover are likely to be carriers of the disease, and they can shed the virus intermittently and cause future outbreaks. Although DNA probes exist to test for PDV, these probes are effective only during the time that the bird is actively shedding the virus, so they are of little use in detecting latent carriers. Other tests can detect the presence of antibodies in the bird's system, which indicates it was exposed to the virus. However, whether this exposure necessarily means the bird is a carrier is unclear. Vaccines are available, which appear to prevent illness but not necessarily infection. This means that a vaccinated parrot will not become sick itself if exposed to the disease, but it might be able to pass the disease on to other birds. If you have an outbreak of Pacheco's, or suspect that you may have carriers in your flock, discuss the pros and cons of vaccination with your veterinarian.

If you have an outbreak, you can do some things to lessen the severity and save lives. However, you must act quickly, because this disease spreads extremely rapidly. The human drug acyclovir can reduce the death rate significantly if given before the birds show signs of serious illness. In birds that have been exposed but are not yet showing clinical signs, powdered acyclovir can be added to the food or administered orally. Birds that are exhibiting early symptoms might be saved by intravenous administration of the drug along with intensive supportive care. Because PDV is a fragile virus outside of its host, good aviary hygiene can help prevent the spread of infection. Spraying cages and floors thoroughly with a disinfectant solution such as chlorhexidine (Nolvasan) before and after sweeping and cleaning can help reduce aerosolization and kill exposed viral particles.

Proventricular dilatation disease, or PDD, is a fatal disease of parrots that currently has no known cause or cure. It is suspected to be a virus, and researchers have discovered a viruslike particle associated

This dropping is filled with undigested seed, which is often a sign of proventricular dilatation disease.

Avoiding PDD

To reduce the likelihood of encountering this disease, follow these precautions:

• Do not purchase a bird from a source that has had a confirmed outbreak.

• Never buy a bird that looks thin or shows any of the symptoms mentioned at right.

• Discuss with your veterinarian the pros and cons of performing radiographs during the new bird exam.

• Always quarantine new arrivals carefully for a minimum of 60 days. (Because PDD can apparently show up years after initial exposure, a 60-day quarantine is obviously no guarantee of safety, but it will allow you time to observe the bird and recognize any clinical symptoms that might be present.)

• Do what you can to support the various nonprofit avian research groups that are raising money to fund PDD research. With a little help, these scientists will one day unravel the mystery of PDD and find ways to keep birds safe.

with the disease. However, it has not yet been classified or proven to be the causative agent. The disease, which damages the nerves in the gastrointestinal tract, was originally discovered in the 1970s in imported macaws and became known as macaw wasting syndrome. When it started to appear in a wide range of other parrot species, it was reported under a variety of different names until finally the research community settled on proventricular dilatation disease.

PDD is a heartbreaking disease that destroys the ventriculus and proventriculus (the muscular stomachs) in the parrot's digestive tract. It causes the bird to starve to death slowly, no matter how much food it consumes. Symptoms include progressive weight loss, vomiting, passing undigested food in the droppings, and crop impactions. In some cases, brain and heart damage occur, causing neurological symptoms such as weakness, lameness, and seizures. An infected bird can show any combination of these symptoms. PDD is especially frustrating because veterinarians have no idea how it transmits. Some aviaries will experience an outbreak where numerous birds die, while others might lose one bird and never have any other losses. Losing one member of a breeding pair is common, yet the mate never develops any disease. Because the movement of the disease is so erratic, predicting how it will manifest or how it can be controlled is nearly impossible. Some researchers now believe that it might have multiple causative agents that must be present at the same time to produce clinical disease or that it might be caused by an autoimmune disorder. Cases have been reported in birds that have been single pets for several years without any exposure to other birds.

Because what causes PDD is not know for certain, birds cannot be tested to find out if they carry it. It is sometimes possible to diagnose in clinically ill birds by performing a biopsy of crop tissue. However, this procedure will not catch all infected birds, and false negative results are not uncommon. A radiograph (X ray) of a bird suspected to have the disease might show an enlarged or congested proventriculus, but several other disease processes could also be responsible. The real problem lies in predicting which apparently healthy birds might carry the disease and pass it on to others. Right now, this is beyond reach. Although the disease can strike almost all parrots (and numerous wild birds), it seems to be especially common in African greys, macaws, and cockatoos.

Although PDD is one of the most dangerous diseases facing parrots today, it is also one of the least understood and least preventable. Much research is being done in the United States and Europe to find answers, but so far researchers are a long way from conquering the problem.

Emergency and First-Aid Treatment

If your birds do fall ill for any reason or if they are injured, their ultimate survival might depend on how quickly and appropriately you react. If a bird appears fluffed up and listless, observe it carefully for a few moments. A sick bird might

- Lose interest in eating
- Become less vocal
- Fluff up its feathers to maintain body heat
- Sit slumped down on its perch

Distinguishing between sick bird posture and a bird that is simply sleepy is important. A healthy but sleepy bird will yawn, fluff up, and squat down on the perch on one leg while it folds the other leg up against its belly. Its eyes might be half-closed, yet it is still alert and will spring to attention if something startles or interests it. A sick bird will fluff up, squat low on the perch *on both legs*, and might have trouble keeping its eyes open. Sometimes the eyes look glassy or unfocused. The bird might also have trouble breathing. If you hear any clicking or wheezing sounds or see its tail bob up and down as it takes a breath, then your bird is probably having respiratory problems.

A change in the color, consistency, or frequency of the droppings can also signal illness. Normal bird droppings consist of three parts. The feces should be well formed and are usually green or brown in color. The urine should be clear. The urates should be white. Runny, unformed feces or urates that are tinted green or yellow might indicate disease, especially when combined with other symptoms.

If you notice any of these symptoms, isolate the bird and call your veterinarian immediately. Keep it

Normal healthy parrot droppings. Birds on a formulated diet may have feces that are brownish instead of green, but the urates should remain white.

warm by placing it into a hospital cage (see Chapter Five) or putting it into a carrier with a heating pad on top. Do not attempt any home treatments except under your veterinarian's supervision. Many people ply their birds with over-the-counter remedies or inappropriate antibiotics and end up worsening the problem or killing the bird. After you gain some experience and work with your veterinarian for a while, he or she might trust you to make a judgment call and administer some drugs in an emergency. However, you should always follow up with an office visit to make sure that the treatment was appropriate and the bird is healing.

Bleeding: Other emergencies include bleeding, fractures, and poisoning. In most cases, your best bet is to keep the bird warm and calm and to transport it immediately to the veterinary clinic. In the case of bleeding, you will need to assess the situation. Healthy parrots have a pretty effective clotting system, but severe loss of blood can lead to shock or death. Sometimes, just placing the bird into a dark, quiet place for a few moments will calm it enough to let its clotting functions kick in.

A few years ago, I entered my aviary late one afternoon and saw blood splattered on the walls, floor, and ceiling. It looked like a scene from a horror movie. I walked through the room in fear, trying to figure out the source of the carnage. Finally, I spotted Charlie, one of my blue-fronted Amazons, perched on the back of a chair. He had escaped from his enclosure and had apparently attempted to remove a toy from the top of a Timneh African grey cage nearby. The Timnehs obviously won the argument, because one of the Amazon's toes now lay severed on the floor of their cage. When I approached Charlie, he greeted me with a cheerful "Hi!" and casually climbed onto my hand as if nothing out of the ordinary had happened. I rushed him to the emergency veterinary clinic for stitches, but the bleeding had long since stopped. Although he had lost a lot of blood, he was calm, alert, and much more interested in the jar of treats on the office counter than he was in his missing toe. He healed quickly and without complications (although he avoids African greys now).

This does not mean you should ignore a bleeding parrot. However, sometimes people see a little blood and panic. They catch the bird, restrain it, and fumble frantically, which only serves to panic the bird and increase its heart rate and blood pressure, making it bleed faster. Before you catch the bird, try to gauge the source and amount of blood. Broken toenails, blood feathers, and chipped beaks might stop bleeding on their own in a minute or two. If not, or if it is a large wound that obviously needs treatment, catch the bird and restrain it gently and calmly. For beaks and nails, a small dab of styptic powder from your first-aid kit should stop the bleeding quickly. For wounds, flush it with hydrogen peroxide to clean it, dab a little povidone-iodine on it to disinfect, and hold gentle pressure on the spot with a clean gauze pad. Because the bird might require sutures, antibiotics, or replacement fluids, you should always contact your veterinarian, even if the bleeding has stopped.

If the bleeding is from a broken blood feather, you might need to pull out the broken feather shaft to stop the bleeding. Immobilize the wing by holding it firmly right above the broken feather, grasp the shaft with a pair of locking needle-nosed pliers, and pull slowly and steadily in the direction of the feather growth. This does hurt, and the bird will not be happy. However, it is sometimes necessary to stop the bleeding. Always be sure to hold the wing bone firmly in a spot near the broken feather. If you hold a spot on the wing several inches away, you increase the risk of breaking the bird's wing when you pull out the feather.

Broken bones: If you suspect your bird has a broken bone, you should get it to the veterinarian immediately to set the break and treat for possible shock. Never try to splint a broken bone on your own. Serious damage to the bone and surrounding tissue can result. This is definitely a job for an experienced avian veterinarian. I once knew a person whose pet bird got caught in the cage bars and broke a wing. It was a pretty simple fracture, but it occurred late at night, so she took the bird to a nearby animal emergency clinic. They admitted they did not see too many birds but assured her they knew what to do. They bandaged it up and sent her home, telling her to come back later that week for a

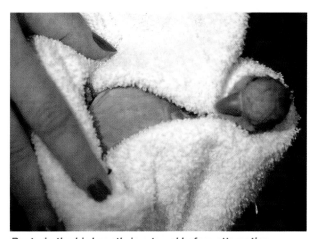

Restrain the bird gently in a towel before attempting any first aid. Do not put pressure on the bird's chest or abdomen during restraint, or you might restrict its breathing.

recheck. Within a day or so, the parrot was obviously not doing well. It would not eat and seemed to be having difficulty breathing.

This time, she found a nearby clinic that specialized in birds which agreed to see her pet right away. The attending veterinarian took one look at the situation and had a fit. It seems that the emergency clinic, in an attempt to immobilize the wing, had taped it so tightly against the bird's body that the crop, chest, and abdomen were all restricted. The poor bird could not eat and could barely breathe. To make matters worse, they had used a sticky tape that damaged all the feathers and caused tissue necrosis in the skin underneath. The bird did survive and eventually recovered completely, but it required weeks of antibiotics and other drugs. The wing had to be rebroken and reset. Keep in mind that a veterinarian caused all this

Blood in the droppings is a possible indication of lead poisoning.

damage due to his lack of avian knowledge. Imagine how much damage you can cause unless you are absolutely certain you know what you are doing!

Poisoning: Two major types of poisonings commonly affect birds: ingestion of toxic substances and exposure to airborne toxins. Less common, but still possible, is contact poisoning, which occurs when a bird sustains skin contact with a poisonous or irritating substance. Parrots are curious creatures and will often pick up and taste anything they come across. They love to chew and have no way of knowing what is safe and what is not. Poisoning is more common in pets that are allowed to roam around the house unsupervised than it is in breeder birds that are typically kept caged. You still must exercise caution, however, to keep poisonous substances out of reach of curious beaks. Sometimes, the problem exists within the cage, as in the case of heavy-metal poisoning from poorly made cages contaminated with zinc or lead. Other times, the birds are able to reach through the bars and grab nearby plants or other objects that are toxic. Signs of poisoning include:
• Lethargy
• Weakness
• Vomiting
• Diarrhea
• Convulsions
• Paralysis

Lead poisoning can sometimes cause blood in the droppings. If you know what the bird has eaten, call your veterinarian or a poison control center immediately for directions. If you are not sure, get the bird to the veterinarian as quickly as possible.

Airborne toxins are a more likely problem for aviary birds. Parrots have extremely complicated and delicate respiratory systems.

A breeder friend of mine lost several large parrots in her home when a new housekeeper unwittingly sprayed an inexpensive room deodorizer near an air vent. The fumes concentrated through the vent and entered the breeding room, killing several birds within moments. My friend heard the screams of the dying birds, rushed in, and realized what had happened. She quickly threw open all the windows (it was in the dead of winter). The incoming fresh air dissipated the fumes and saved the remaining birds. A horrible tragedy could have been averted if the housekeeper had only known.

Another source for airborne toxin is Teflon and some other brands of nonstick cookware. When overheated, these pans give off polytetrafluoroethylene (PTFE) gas, which is odorless, colorless, and rapidly fatal to birds. I tossed out all my nonstick cookware after I got involved with birds and now use nothing but stainless steel. Teflon might also show up on irons and ironing board covers, burner pans, and space heaters and as a coating on some brands of heat lamps. If you use any of these items, use them far away from the birds, venti-

Poison Control

A wide variety of gases and fumes can cause death. These include
• Paint
• Chemical fumes
• Car exhaust
• Insecticides
• Cleaning products
• Aerosol sprays

late the room or use an exhaust fan to draw the air away from the aviary, and do not allow high heat levels to occur. If a bird is exposed to PTFE gas, death usually occurs rapidly. If the bird is still alive, rush it to a veterinarian as quickly as possible. Sometimes a combination of steroids, antibiotics, and fluids will save a bird that has experienced only minimal exposure.

Other Diseases

Dozens of other diseases can affect parrots. However, the ones discussed above are the most common and some of the most deadly. Viruses, bacteria, fungi, and parasites are just a few of the organisms that cause disease in humans and animals alike. Parrots are also prone to most of the same degenerative diseases that afflict mammals, such as diabetes, arthritis, cardiovascular disease, and cancer. Luckily, comparative disease studies allow advances made in animal medicine to benefit humans and vice versa.

Chapter Eight

Avian Reproduction (The Birds, Not the Bees)

Without a basic understanding of the mechanics of breeding, the aviculturist would have difficulty recognizing when and where things go wrong. Infertility can be caused by disease or dysfunction of either the male or female reproductive tracts or by improper breeding positions in healthy, normal birds. A complete lack of breeding behavior might stem from incompatibility, stress, or malnutrition. A multitude of factors work together to create a harmonious and successful breeding pair. If anything in the equation is missing, then reproduction is unlikely.

The Female Reproductive System

Like her human counterpart, a female parrot's reproductive tract consists of ovaries, oviducts, and a vagina. In birds, however, the right ovary and oviduct fail to develop after hatching and become atrophied and nonfunctional. The left ovary, which is situated near the left kidney, is attached to the abdominal wall by a thin ligament known as the mesovarian. The ovary has two functions: to produce the female hormones estrogen and progesterone and to produce ova. The female ovary will also produce a small amount of the male hormone testosterone. The ovary itself is made up of two parts, the medulla and the cortex. The medulla is made up of smooth muscle, nerves, and blood vessels. The cortex, which covers the medulla, contains the cells that will eventually turn into ova. The ovary of a female parrot may contain up to 12,000 of these cells (primary oocytes), although only a small percentage will actually grow into the primary follicles that will someday become eggs. The primary follicles are the oocytes and their membranous covering that are easily visible on the surface of a mature ovary. In immature birds, these follicles are difficult to see with the naked eye.

Egg Production

During breeding season, the ovary of a mature bird will increase greatly in size as several primary follicles mature and fill with yolk. About two hours before ovulation, the oocyte undergoes the first of two divisions and forms what is called the first polar body and the secondary oocyte. These contain only half the normal number of chromosomes. After this division, ovulation occurs. The follicle splits open, and the secondary oocyte is engulfed by the oviduct. Ovulation also causes smooth muscle contractions in the oviduct, which will move the oocyte along through the oviduct.

Once in the oviduct, the second division of the oocyte begins, which forms the ovum and the second polar body. During this division, the oocyte is in the first section of the oviduct, which is known as the infundibulum. This is where fertilization will take place if sperm cells (spermatozoa) are present. During fertilization, the sperm penetrates the ovum and completes the number of chromosomes. In birds, the mother's chromosomes determine the sex of the offspring, whereas in humans and other mammals it is determined by the father. The ovum passes through the infundibulum in about 15 minutes. During this time a thin,

A mature avian ovary showing developing follicles.

dense layer of albumen forms around the yolk. Connected to this layer are two thick twisted strands of albumen, known as chalazae. Their function is to anchor and suspend the yolk between the two ends of the egg. Once this process is complete, the egg passes into the next section of the oviduct, which is a glandular area known as the magnum.

In the magnum, the body begins the process of covering the yolk with albumen, which is what people commonly call egg whites. Albumen is made up primarily of protein and can act as a source of protein for the growing embryo. It also has antibacterial properties and helps protect the growing embryo. Once the layers of albumen are deposited (about a three-hour process), the egg passes into the next section of the

During the period of eggshell calcification, the hen must replace her total blood plasma calcium level approximately every 15 minutes! This is why it is absolutely critical that breeding hens are fed a high-quality diet that supplies plenty of calcium and other nutrients well in advance of breeding season, so that they can build up their stores of calcium.

oviduct. This is a narrow area known as the isthmus. It is here that the shell membranes are formed from keratin and deposited around the ovum and albumen. This process takes about an hour and a half. The egg has two shell membranes, an inner membrane and an outer one. The outer membrane will lie directly under the eggshell once it has formed. The inner membrane lies just below the outer one. The air sac of the growing egg is situated between the two membranes.

Once the membranes are complete, the egg moves into the uterus, which is also known as the shell gland in birds. It will remain here for the next 20 hours or so as the eggshell forms. During the first five to eight hours, uterine glands add water and minerals that double the weight of the albumen. Over the next 15 hours, the uterus withdraws calcium from the hen's blood, and calcification of the shell begins. To provide sufficient calcium for the shell, female birds are able to draw calcium from a specialized bone structure called medullary bone. Although many of the bones in a parrot's body are filled with air sacs (these are called pneumatic bones), female birds can deposit extra calcium stores into certain bones (such as their femur, or leg bone) and mobilize it quickly when needed for egg production.

The eggshell itself consists of three layers: the shell membranes, the testa, and the cuticle. The testa is the primary layer. It consists of a

Parrot eggs vary greatly in size. This picture shows (in ascending size) a tiny Pacific parrotlet egg, a Goffin's cockatoo egg, a Congo African grey egg, a green-winged macaw egg, and a grade A extra-large chicken egg for size comparison.

fine matrix of protein fibers that is covered with a thick layer of calcite (a crystalline form of calcium carbonate). The testa has thousands of pores that allow moisture and gases to diffuse into or out of the egg. These pores allow oxygen into the egg but can also serve as an entryway for dangerous pathogens.

The final layer, known as the cuticle, is a thin film of protein that covers the testa. It helps to regulate the water loss through the shell and also acts as a barrier to bacteria. Once the shell is completed, the egg passes into the vagina and on through to the cloaca, where it is ready to be laid. Although the hen has had no control of the process up to this point, she is able to retain the egg in the cloaca for a while until she is ready to lay. This allows her time to return to her nest instead of simply popping out the egg during flight or at some other inopportune moments.

The Male Reproductive System

Although a hen can produce an egg without a male, it will of course be infertile. The male reproductive system forms the spermatozoa, which fertilize the egg and contribute half the chromosomes to the embryo. A male parrot's reproductive tract consists of testes, epididymis, and the ductus deferens.

The yellowish-white testes of a mature male parrot resemble a kidney bean.

Parrots lack some of the sex glands and structures present in humans and other mammals, including the prostate gland, seminal vesicle, and a penis.

The testes are paired organs that are situated in the abdominal cavity in front of and slightly above the kidneys. In most parrots, the testes are oblong or bean shaped and creamy white in color, although in cockatoos and a few other parrots they are dark gray or black. They will vary greatly in size, depending on the bird's level of maturity and sexual activity. During breeding season, a mature male's testes can become enlarged up to 300 times their normal (nonbreeding) size. The testes are composed primarily of structures called seminiferous tubules. These tubules are lined with cells that multiply and grow to form sperm cells.

Between the tubules are specialized cells that produce the male sex hormone testosterone, which is responsible for a variety of secondary sexual characteristics. These characteristics include male sexual behaviors such as aggression and territorialism.

After the sperm form, they flow from the testes and through a short system of ductules known as the epididymis. In mammals, sperm are stored in the epididymis while they go through a process of maturation and develop mobility. In birds, this step does not occur until the sperm reach the next section of the reproductive tract, which is known as the ductus deferens. It appears that the epididymis in birds is vestigial, which means it no longer serves a clearly defined purpose.

The ductus deferens serve as the storage organs for sperm, and this is where the sperm undergo the final process of maturity. These long, convoluted tubes run from each testis, parallel along the ureter, and into the cloaca. Just before they end at the cloaca, they form a small, saclike area that terminates with an erectile papilla, which is an ejaculatory duct. When the bird ejaculates,

it expels about one-half to two-thirds of the contents of both ductus deferens. Sexually active birds need from one to four days to replenish the supply.

Doing the Deed

Because the entire reproductive tract of both male and female parrots is internal and because male parrots lack a penis, one of the most common questions inexperienced bird people ask is "How do they do it?" In reality, they do it in much the same way as mammals but with a few minor differences. In most parrot species, a female that is willing to mate will crouch down low on the perch, droop her wings, and lift her tail. The male will either climb onto her back or stand next to her and place one foot onto her back. He then curves his tail under hers so that their cloacal openings are aligned. At this point, both birds slightly evert their cloacal tissue, and the male ejaculates and deposits his sperm onto the hen's cloacal tissue. This process has been dubbed the *cloacal kiss.*

If the mating was successful, the sperm will travel up the female's cloaca to her vagina, where they can be stored, sometimes for several days or weeks, until she is ready to ovulate. When she does ovulate, the sperm move from the vagina, up through the oviduct, and into the infundibulum within a period of minutes. No one is sure how the sperm

> **Did You Know? . . .**
> Unlike human sperm, avian sperm can remain viable for many days, perhaps even weeks, after ejaculation. For this reason, birds are able to produce multiple fertile eggs after just one mating.

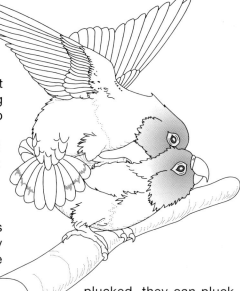

During mating, the hen will crouch low on the perch and lift her tail. The male wraps his tail under hers to align their cloacas.

survive so long in the vagina or what causes them to be released during ovulation, but the system seems to work pretty well most of the time.

With the exception of actual infertility, most of the problems that do occur are external. Because mating requires a certain amount of skill, balance, and dexterity to perform the cloacal kiss, some birds just don't get it right, especially young and inexperienced types. I've seen youngsters attempting to mate in some very strange positions, usually with their cloacas nowhere near each other. Improper technique is most common in hand-raised domestic parrots. They are sometimes sexually naïve because they were not around their parents and flock mates long enough to learn the facts of life from a parrot perspective. With a little practice and patience, they will often make wonderful breeders, although this does seem to vary by species. Sometimes placing the slow learners next to an experienced pair helps so that they can watch and take notes.

Some breeders will pluck all the feathers from around the birds' vents, reasoning that this gives them better contact. I've heard this does help canaries and other small perching birds, but I'm not convinced it would make a great deal of difference in parrots, which have a lot more dexterity. If birds want the feathers plucked, they can pluck them themselves.

Another common problem is poor perching materials. Thin, slippery, or widely spaced perches can make it difficult for the hen to keep a solid grip. This is especially critical in large, heavy-bodied species like macaws and cockatoos. Distractions and sudden loud noises in the aviary will serve as a deterrent to breeding. On more than one occasion, I've cheerfully breezed into my aviary only to be greeted by the loud thump of a male in coitus interruptus being dumped onto the cage floor because I've startled the hen and caused her to bolt upright. During breeding season, keep unannounced visits to a minimum. I usually whistle or call to the birds from the next room, then pause before I enter, which gives them a moment to, ahem, finish what they were doing.

Is It Really Love?

The final point to consider is whether or not the birds really like each other. Sometimes the chemistry just isn't there. No matter what you do, they just aren't going to produce. Period. If you have a nonproducing pair, you will need to observe them carefully to determine what's going on. This is where a small, closed-circuit camera system really comes in handy. Gauging behavior while you're in the same room is hard because most parrots will stop whatever they're doing and focus on you. If you have a camera system, set it up to record the pair in question. If you don't, you'll have to resort to sneaking up and hiding behind a door or something. Watch the birds for several minutes at a time, as often as possible over a few days. How do they interact with each other? Here are a few points to consider:

• Do they fight a lot? Some species, especially Amazons and macaws, do a lot of minor quibbling and beak dueling during breeding season, but these sessions are interspersed with lots of cuddling and cooing. If one bird is frequently chasing the other, however, or keeping it away from food and water, it is probably an abusive relationship. If you notice any signs of serious aggression or injury, or if one bird seems genuinely frightened of the other, then separate them immediately. This relationship is probably doomed.

• Do they spend time interacting? Even strongly bonded pairs might like a little time alone, but they will usually gravitate back to each other after a short while. Playing, mutual preening, and perching side by side are signs of a happy couple.

• How do they react when food is offered? Bonded pairs usually share food, including coveted treats, pretty amicably. One of my macaw hens has a hard time opening Brazil nuts, but she loves them. When I put Brazil nuts into the dish, the male will take one, crack it open, and hand it to the hen before he takes one for himself.

• How do they interact with nearby birds? Sometimes the problem is with the neighbors. Hormonal male Amazons and cockatoos are especially prone to spending huge chunks of their day hanging on the cage bars, screaming threats at all their perceived rivals, while the hen sits alone and bored on the perch. In a case like this, draping part of the cage with a cover or hanging visual barriers might restore some peace and harmony.

If your observations uncover some problems, you might try to change the surroundings and see if anything improves. Visual barriers, larger cages, extra food dishes, or a change in lighting might put a little romance into the union. If not, your only real choice is to break up the pair and place them with new mates. Of course, be sure that you have allowed them enough time to bond before you make any snap decisions. Parrot love doesn't always happen overnight. Give your birds several months or a year together before you decide that it isn't going to work.

Finally, although this might seem obvious, be sure that you have a true pair (male and female). I once got a proven pair of greys from a good friend who was in poor health and reducing her breeding stock. They settled in quickly, seemed genuinely fond of each other, and began to mate enthusiastically, although no eggs appeared. About a year later, I discovered that I actually had two males. It seems that my friend had two proven pairs of greys, and, at some point, the birds escaped from their cages. Her assistant caught them and shoved them back in but, unfortunately, made a slight error in putting the right birds into the right cage. Her remaining pair (which was happily working the nest box) was the two hens. My friend was horrified and embarrassed, but we made a quick swap and had a good laugh over the whole incident.

The point of the story is that both sets of birds continued to mate and act bonded even though they were same-sex pairs. Apparently, they had been caged near each other for a long time and were friendly, so when the switch occurred, they shrugged it off and got on with their lives, which included copulation and nesting activity. They were, of course, happy to be reunited with their original mates and are back to producing chicks. Just because you see parrots mating, it is no guarantee that they're of the opposite sex. Bisexuality is not uncommon in

Sometimes hormonal male parrots will spend much of their time in territory disputes with nearby birds and ignore their mates.

parrots. A sexually stimulated parrot will attempt to mate with just about anything—animal, vegetable, or mineral. My pet cockatoo once became so enamored of a certain large rubber toy that we had to remove it from his cage because he was becoming aggressive and unpredictable.

Until you see chicks in the nest box, don't assume that you have a true pair, no matter how the birds act toward each other. Plenty of dishonest people out there will try to pass off same-sex or infertile birds as proven breeding pairs. Even if you trust the person you got them from, mix-ups do occur or a recent undetected illness could have caused fertility problems. If you have any doubts, resex them. It might save you a lot of time and aggravation in the long run.

Chapter Nine

Incubation: Count Your Chicks Before They Hatch

In a perfect world, the parent birds will tend their eggs carefully and feed and nurture the newborn chicks on through weaning. Sometimes things even go this smoothly in real life. Unfortunately, sometimes it does not. The parents abandon the nest, eat the eggs, or brutalize the newly hatched chicks. If any of this occurs, you will need to be prepared to step in and become an instant nanny.

Even when things are going well, some folks decide to remove the eggs to encourage the hen to produce more. Often, parrots will attempt to replace a clutch that disappears, so pulling the first batch of eggs might result in the pair returning to the nest and laying a second batch, or *double clutching.* Keep in mind that this puts a terrible strain onto the hen's body, however. So please don't let a desire for increased production lead you to practices that compromise your bird's health. In any case, if you're breeding birds, you'll need to under-

stand the principles and methods of incubation, which are basically the processes that turn a fertile egg into a live chick.

Nest Box Maintenance

Chapter Four discussed the various styles of nest boxes and mentioned some suggestions for substrate. No matter what you have chosen to use, you must keep it clean. Because wooden nest boxes are impossible to disinfect properly, you should change them every year at the end of breeding season. Change substrates after every clutch or more often as needed. Sometimes my macaws hatch big clutches, and the nest box gets really disgusting long before I'm ready to remove the chicks. When this happens, I'll quickly place the chicks into a cardboard box, scoop the worst of the crud into a garbage can, put in fresh bedding, and return the chicks to the nest. Of course, not all pairs will be so tolerant of this kind of interference, so use good judgment. Actually, my birds seem to appreciate the maid service.

Frequently changing the substrate has a benefit beyond simple cleanliness and safety. I use fir bark chunks, and several of my hens feel the need to chew it into powder before they lay eggs. Putting new bark in for them to chew can stimulate breeding behavior. On the other hand, some hens like to remove the substrate completely and lay their eggs onto the bare floor of the box. This can be a problem since the eggs are not properly cushioned and can roll around and crack. For pairs that do this, I try to keep adding bark faster than they can throw it out. Sometimes I win, sometimes the birds win. You can also try a different type of substrate or offer clean, carefully disinfected tree branches that the hen can chew to her heart's content.

Inspections

The issue of nest box inspections is an area of disagreement among some aviculturists. Basically two kinds of breeders exist when it comes to nest box inspections. The first kind spends so much time rummaging around in the box that the hen thinks she may have to start feeding them. I was like this in my earlier days. The second kind refuses ever to inspect their nest boxes, convinced that the birds would be so psychologically traumatized by the intrusion that they will never breed again. I have a dear friend like this. When I asked her if she had some words of wisdom to contribute to this book, she said, "Yeah. Tell 'em to stay out of the boxes!"

In truth, periodic nest box inspections are necessary. However, the frequency and timing should depend on the pair's temperament. Some species are so nervous and high-strung (wild-caught cockatoos, for example) that an intrusion might cause them to destroy eggs or kill chicks. Others are pretty laid back and don't care too much about what you do or when you do it. I leave my nest boxes up year-round. Several pairs are nest box divers that disappear into the box as soon as I enter the room. Even when they are not breeding, I feel it's necessary to peek into the box occasionally to

Use common sense when inspecting nest boxes, or the parents might destroy the eggs or desert the nest.

make sure that these adults look alive and well. To get the birds used to the inspections, try following a few rules of mine:

• Always knock gently on the box first to let them know what's happening.
• Take a look and then close up the box quickly.
• Always drop a special treat in their dish afterwards so they associate the inspection with goodies.
• To move the hen gently off the nest so you can candle eggs or examine chicks, use a small square of thin plywood, which also acts as a shield to prevent the parents from attacking either the chicks or you.

Candling Eggs

When you do find eggs in the nest box, you have a few choices. You can, of course, just close the box and see what happens in the next 30 days or so. Most breeders prefer to candle the eggs to see if they are fertile. Candling is a method of determining fertility in eggs by shining a bright light through them. Although you can do this with a flashlight, it will not work anywhere nearly as well as a special candling light. Candling lights are designed to throw off a very powerful and concentrated beam, which does a much better job of illuminating an egg's interior. Some brands are designed with long, flexible shafts so you can bend them to inspect eggs right in the nest without ever picking them up and handling them. Jarring the eggs can kill the developing embryo, so the less you handle them, the better.

Parrot eggs do not usually start to show visible signs of fertility until several days after they have been laid. Do not bother candling a brand new egg unless you have a reason to suspect the egg might be cracked or punctured from the parent's toenails. (How to repair these will be explained later.) A fertile egg will begin to show the development of tiny blood vessels after about four or five days of incubation. These will first appear as a network of faint spidery red veins, which will grow and become more prominent as development progresses. At the large end of the egg, you will see the air cell, which will get larger as the chick grows. An infertile egg has no blood vessels and will just show a diffuse yellowish glow from the yolk when candled. If an egg was fertile but the embryo has died, you will see a patchy or solid ring of blood (called a blood ring) that lacks the tiny spreading blood vessels. This hap-

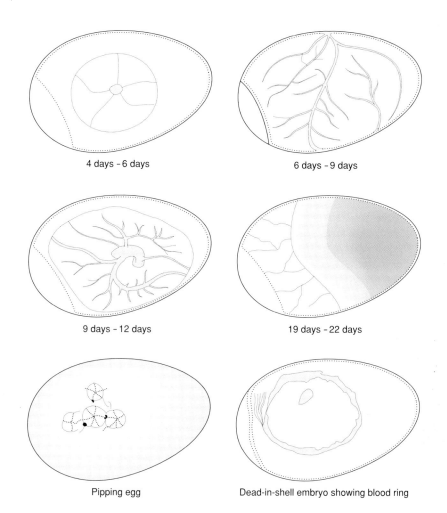

4 days – 6 days

6 days – 9 days

9 days – 12 days

19 days – 22 days

Pipping egg

Dead-in-shell embryo showing blood ring

As the embryo develops, the egg will become more difficult to candle as the growing chick fills the shell. A few days before hatch, the air cell will enlarge to allow the hatching chick to make the transition to breathing air. These illustrations are approximations. Actual development may vary due to species, incubator temperature, or other factors.

pens when the developing veins die off and clot. These eggs are called dead in shell. If the eggs do not show signs of fertility after ten days, they are probably clear, or infertile, assuming that the hen has been incubating them. At this point, I usually pull the clutch and place it into the incubator, just to be sure that the lack of development is not caused by improper incubation. Some clueless hens will sit in the nest box and stare at the eggs but never actually sit on them.

If the eggs still do not show development after five or six days of artificial incubation, you can discard them. They were most likely infertile but could have suffered an early embryonic failure due to disease or rough handling by the parents. Remember, however, giving young and inexperienced hens ample opportunity to learn proper parenting skills is always a good idea. You should leave the first few clutches with her for a full incubation period, even if it means sacrificing fertile eggs. If she still does not incubate properly, or if she refuses to care for newly hatched chicks, then you will have to take over those duties. Sometimes, re-pairing a young hen with a more experienced male will work because he can teach her the parenting skills she lacks.

If you have a hen that never does learn how to raise chicks, you might consider removing her from your breeding program, because chicks that are hatched and at least partially raised by the parents are often healthier and more emotionally stable than incubator-reared chicks. Of course, with the relative rarity of some species these days, this may not be an option.

Parental Incubation

If you do have fertile eggs in the nest box and the parents are apparently doing their job, then you can give them a little privacy for a while. Continuing inspections is not necessary unless you see a sign that something has gone wrong, like both parents being out of the box for long periods of time. If you know roughly when the eggs were laid, you can calculate the approximate hatch date. Most parrot eggs hatch after about 24 to 28 days of incubation, give or take a few days. I check the box and candle the eggs again about a week before they are due to hatch. If everything looks okay, I usually just leave them alone and let nature take its course. Once the chicks begin to hatch, I take a quick peek to make sure that the parents are feeding them. However, I try to give the parents and their new family as much privacy as possible. After you get to know your pairs, you will learn which ones to trust as parents and which ones bear watching.

Artificial Incubation

If you decide to incubate the eggs artificially, you will have better hatchability if you allow the parents to incubate for the first two weeks before you move the eggs to the incubator. This works well for pairs that will sit on the eggs but not feed their chicks. Of course, if the parents won't sit at all, you'll have to take your chances from day one. Before you pull the eggs, get your incubator set up and running, and allow several hours for the temperature and humidity to stabilize. When you're ready to move the eggs, wash your hands carefully so that you don't transfer bacteria or other pathogens onto the shell. Remember, parrot eggs are extremely sensitive to vibration, so handle them slowly and gently. I usually make a cradle of soft facial tissues in a shallow bowl and nestle the eggs carefully into the tissues to carry them.

Repairing Damaged Eggs

Before you place the eggs into the incubator, take a moment to inspect them. If the eggs are dirty from being in the nest, you can wipe them gently with a piece of gauze moistened with sterile water. Remember, the eggs are porous, so never use any soaps or chemicals to clean them. While using your candling light, check the eggs carefully for cracks or small holes from the parent's toenails. Even tiny hairline cracks can admit bacteria and will affect the moisture loss from the egg. You will need to repair them if the egg is to survive.

Temperature

During artificial incubation, accurate temperature and humidity control are absolutely critical for success. I've had the best luck using an incubator temperature of 99.5°F (37.5°C) with a wet-bulb temperature of 82°F to 84°F (27.8°C to 28.9°C) at 50 to 54 percent relative humidity. If the temperature falls more than 1°F (0.5°C) below this for an extended

How to Repair Eggs

The best substance for repairing eggs is nontoxic, water-soluble white glue, like Elmer's Glue-All. Take a small paintbrush, and soak it in chlorhexidine solution for about 10 minutes to disinfect it. Then gently paint a little glue over the crack or hole to seal it. You might need to add a second or third coat. Do not smear glue all over the egg—just cover the damaged area.

If the egg is badly damaged and has shell pieces missing, saving it is still sometimes possible if the shell membrane is intact. You can use a small piece of sterile gauze, tissue, or Scotch tape as a patch. Place glue carefully around the outer edges of the hole, and gently press a piece of gauze over it. Brush glue over the gauze, covering the hole completely. If you use scotch tape, place a tiny piece over the hole, then brush glue around the edges. Once it dries, add a second or third coat to thicken and stiffen it.

If the hole is over the air cell, you will need to remove this patch when the chick is ready to hatch. When the time comes, dampen the patch with sterile water and pull it off carefully. Eggs that are badly cracked or damaged often do not survive, but it is certainly worth a try.

The biggest danger is from bacterial contamination. Disinfect your hands and any equipment carefully!

time, the chicks might be delayed in hatching or be weak. If the temperature stays even slightly higher (above 99.9°F or 37.7°C), the chicks can die or have difficulty absorbing the yolk sac. Brief temperature fluctuations usually won't hurt, like the cooldown that occurs when you open the incubator to candle the eggs. In fact, a few short cool-downs a day might even enhance hatchability because it more closely replicates the natural temperature changes that occur as the hen moves on and off the eggs. Keep in mind that I'm referring to minor, short-term fluctuations. In general, keep the temperature as accurate as possible to ensure healthy hatches.

Humidity Control

Humidity control is just as important. Humidity regulates the moisture loss from within the egg. If the humidity level falls too low, the egg will lose moisture and dehydrate, which will cause hatching problems or even kill the chick, depending on the amount of moisture lost. If the humidity is too high, the egg will not be able to rid itself of excess moisture and expand its air cell. The chick will not be able to breathe. Remember, the wet-bulb thermometer reading on your incubator is just as critical as the dry-bulb reading. In order to get an accurate wet-bulb reading, you must keep the wick reservoir filled with water and make sure the wick stays wet at all times. You can also use an electronic gauge, but make sure you get one

that is accurate. To maintain the proper humidity level in the incubator, you might need to adjust the ambient humidity in the room. For example, if you live in a hot, humid climate and the relative humidity indoors is 75 percent, the incubator cannot remain at the required 50 to 54 percent level unless you run a dehumidifier in the room. On the other hand, during Chicago winters, for instance, indoor humidity can drop to as low as 10 to 12 percent, so I often run a room humidifier to give the incubator a boost. Although high-quality incubators are less sensitive to ambient conditions, some external help might be needed.

In theory, a developing egg needs to lose somewhere between 13 to 18 percent of its total weight between the day incubation commences and the day that the chick begins the external pip. There are mathematical formulas that you can use to calculate the desired weight loss trend and adjust your humidity levels accordingly. This requires weighing the eggs daily and is a rather complex process. I'm not going to discuss the egg-weighing method here because, truthfully, I know of very few aviculturists who actually use the procedure. We do not yet have enough data on the 300+ parrot species in aviculture to predict the optimum weight loss for each species. Besides, this method requires a lot of handling of the eggs, and I believe that opens the door for more problems than it solves. In my experience, and based on interviews I've done with other breeders, I think you'll have few problems if you maintain the 99.5°F (37.5°C) temperature and the 82°F to 84°F (27.8°C to 28.9°C) wet-bulb temperature.

Egg Position

Once you have stabilized the incubator, the time has come to put the eggs in. When I place them into the incubator trays, I set each egg onto a small square of sterile gauze. This cushions them a little and helps prevent them from rolling around. The best position for a parrot egg is on its side, with the rounded (larger) end of the egg just slightly elevated. Although this is pretty much the natural position that an egg will lie in, you can bunch up the gauze a little to keep the end elevated and to stop it from rocking back and forth during egg turning. The wide end of the egg is where the air cell is located, and that is where the chick's head needs to end up during hatching. If the pointed end is elevated, the chick might become malpositioned and have difficulty hatching.

To keep bacteria levels in the incubator down, I add chlorhexidine solution (Nolvasan) to the water reservoir at a dilution of 20cc Nolvasan to 1 gallon (3.8 L) of water. This is a perfectly safe disinfectant and will help stop many common pathogens from setting up housekeeping. Do not ever use any other chemicals in the unit because the fumes they emit can permeate the egg and kill the chick.

Once the incubator's humidity and temperature are stabilized, place the eggs gently onto a piece of sterile gauze in the incubator tray.

Once the eggs are nestled safely in the incubator, you will need to monitor them carefully to ensure that the temperature and humidity are remaining where they belong. Always make sure to keep the water reservoirs filled, and check the vent positioning. Never close the vents completely, or the egg will suffocate due to lack of oxygen entering the unit. You can candle the eggs every day if you like to watch the chick develop. As the incubation period progresses, the egg will become harder to candle. The growing chick fills up the shell. However, you should still be able to see red blood vessels, especially along the membrane that separates the chick from the air cell.

Although the turning mechanism on your incubator should be rotating the eggs every hour or so, you should rotate them manually once or twice a day. This prevents the growing embryo from sticking to the membrane and dying. To do so, gently roll the egg 180 degrees so that the section that was resting on the gauze is now facing up. Some breeders mark their eggs with an X on one side and an O on the other in soft pencil so that they can easily visualize the degree to turn. Always roll them sideways, not end over end, and make sure the large end stays slightly elevated.

About three or four days before hatching, the air cell of the egg will appear very prominent and might appear to change shape. This is called drawdown or internal pip. This means that the chick is breaking through the inner shell membrane to move its head into the air cell and is beginning to breathe air. At this point, you should shut off the automatic egg turner and stop rotating the egg, or the chick might become disoriented. If you have a separate hatching unit, place the egg into there and increase the wet-bulb temperature to about 92°F to 94°F (33.3°C to 34.4°C) (about 80 percent relative humidity).

You can use the incubator as a hatching unit, of course. However, a problem arises if you have several eggs at different stages of development. Younger eggs that haven't pipped yet will still need to be turned and cannot be kept at such a high humidity. If you do not have two separate units, you'll have to improvise. You will need to shut off the turner because of the hatching egg, but you can continue to rotate the younger eggs manually several times a day. If they are well along in the incubation process, turning them 180 degrees four to six times a day should be adequate.

Keep the humidity setting at regular incubation levels, but place the hatching egg into a Ziploc plastic bag with one or two cotton balls moistened with sterile water. (Do not let the egg touch the cotton balls or it will become chilled.) Leave the bag partly open, or poke a few air holes into it. The plastic bag will hold in the humidity, effectively raising the humidity level for the hatching chick, without affecting the younger eggs. Open the bag completely a few times a day so that the humidity doesn't build up too high, and keep a close eye on what's happening. Keep in mind that this is a very crude method. If you are going to be doing a lot of egg incubation, you should consider buying a second incubator or hatcher.

Once the chick has made the internal pip, you should be able to see its head moving around in the air cell. Some chicks are very vocal at this point, so you might even hear a faint peeping. Move the egg around as little as possible during this stage because you might disorient the chick and make its hatch more difficult. Within a day or so, you will see a star-shaped crack appear somewhere over the air cell. This is the external pip, which means the chick is beginning the arduous process of chipping its way out of the shell. The chick does this by chipping at the shell with its egg tooth, which is a hard, sharp projection on the tip of the upper beak. This egg tooth separates from the beak and falls off when the chick is a few weeks old. Hatching is a lot of work, and the chick will take frequent naps. So don't be alarmed if you don't detect any sign of movement for a while. Most parrots complete the hatching process within a day or two of external pip but can sometimes take three or even four days. If you don't see signs of progress after two or three days or if the chick sounds distressed (you'll hear a frantic-sounding peep), you might have to assist the hatch.

Assisted Hatching

Probably the biggest mistake most breeders make is attempting to assist too early. Chicks can take up to four days from external pip to make it out of the shell. Attempting to yank them out before they are ready can weaken or kill them. If you can see the chick moving around when you candle the egg and if it does not sound distressed, you are probably better off leaving it alone for another 24 hours. The exception is when the chick is malpositioned in

the egg. Sometimes a chick gets turned around and winds up with its head in the small end of the egg. If the external pip (the star-shaped crack) is not somewhere over the air cell, then the chick will need hatching assistance.

Before you begin, gather your supplies. You will need the following:
- A soft, clean towel to work on
- Tweezers
- Sterile cotton swabs (Q-tips)
- Sterile water or sterile saline solution
- Povidone-iodine (Betadine)
- Styptic powder (Kwik-Stop)
- Candling light
- Heating pad
- Electrolyte solution (Pedialyte)
- Tiny, fine-tipped artist's paintbrushes

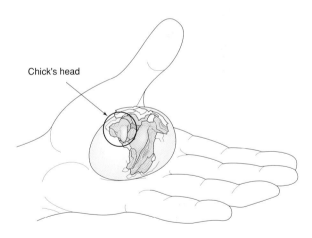

Chick's head

When assisting a hatch, it's important to locate and uncover the chick's head so that it can breathe. However, never attempt to peel away any shell or membrane if active blood vessels are present.

A normal hatch. This chick is almost ready to join the world.

Because this procedure is akin to surgery, observe a high level of cleanliness. Scrub your hands thoroughly, including under your nails. Turn the heating pad to low, and place the towel on top of it. You don't need a lot of heat, but a little extra warmth will prevent the chick from chilling during the procedure. Start by candling the egg to get an idea how the chick is positioned. By using the tweezers, *carefully* chip a piece of shell from a spot over the air cell. Breaching the shell initially is difficult. However, do not put too much pressure onto the tweezers, or you run the risk of slipping and stabbing the chick underneath. Once you have broken into the air cell, you should see the chick's head, although it might be covered with a white, papery membrane. If the chick is malpositioned and has pipped at the small end of the egg, carefully remove a bit of shell at that spot

also. Your goal here is to locate the chick's head and free it so that it can breathe. Before you proceed any further, dip a cotton swap into sterile water, and dampen the membrane. It should turn clear. Gently begin to push aside or peel away the membrane covering the chick's head. If you see red blood vessels in the membrane, the chick is not ready to hatch, and you should stop immediately. Place the egg into a Ziploc bag, and return it to the hatcher. You can try again in a few hours if the blood vessels have receded.

If you do not see blood vessels, you can move ahead. Continue to dampen the membrane and slowly peel away bits of shell. Again, if you see any sign of active blood vessels, stop immediately. If you accidentally hit a vessel and the chick begins to bleed, dab some styptic powder onto the spot with a cotton swab or with the tip of the paintbrush. Once the chick's head is uncovered and it can breathe, it is out of immediate danger. Sometimes this is all the help it needed, and it will push out of the shell by itself. If it seems very weak, you can place a drop of Pedialyte into its mouth with the tip of the paintbrush, then put it back into the hatcher for a while so that it can warm up and rest. If it does not come out on its own within the next hour or so, you will need to remove some more shell. Before you do so, lift the chick's head and try to get a look at its navel area for signs of an unabsorbed yolk sac. Chicks draw the remainder of the yolk into their abdomens before hatching. If the process is not complete, then it still is not ready to hatch. Put it back and try again later.

Once you do get the little guy out, dab a bit of Betadine onto its navel to disinfect and help heal the area, and place it into the brooder. If the navel area is bleeding at all, place a little styptic powder onto the spot, cushion the chick on a piece of gauze, and place it back into the hatcher for a few hours. If the umbilical area is open or if the yolk sac is still protruding from the abdomen, place the chick into the hatcher and call your veterinarian. A severely protruding yolk sac requires medical intervention, including stitches and/or surgery. If only a tiny bit is sticking out, it may absorb on its own. However, you should never tug on it or try to remove it in any way, or the chick will bleed to death.

Power Failures

One of the most frustrating and least-preventable problems associated with artificial incubation is a power failure. If you have a portable generator, make sure that it produces the proper current, or you run the risk of damaging the sensitive electronics in your incubator. Some backup power supplies designed for computers will operate an incubator for a few hours, but the quality and capacity of these varies greatly. Check carefully to be certain that yours will work with your equipment. If you have questions, do not hesitate to call the manufacturer.

Another nifty little device you can use is called a power failure alarm. You plug it into any regular wall outlet. If the power is interrupted for more than ten seconds or so, it sounds a loud, beeping alarm, and a red LED light flashes. I keep it plugged in near my bed, and it wakes me when we have one of those middle-of-the night outages that I might otherwise sleep through. It's designed to ignore those frequent few-second power blips that occur during storms and mess up all your clocks. However, it will roust you quickly when things really shut down. They are available by mail order. (See "Resource Guide.")

If you are not lucky enough to have a generator or other alternate power supply, you will have to do your best to keep the eggs warm. First, call the power company and see if they can tell you when the problem will be corrected. A 10- or 15-minute outage will not matter at all. However, you should unplug the incubator so that it isn't damaged by a surge when the power comes back on. I know this sounds stupid, but don't forget to plug it back in. I actually forgot one sleep-deprived night, but luckily the eggs survived.

If it appears that the power is going to be out for an hour or more, begin by closing the vent and covering the incubator with a blanket. This will hold in the heat for an hour or more, depending on the size and amount of insulation in your unit. Obviously, a heavy, wooden-cabinet model will retain heat longer than a small, molded-plastic unit. If the heat is still not on after an hour, you should try to add some heat to the unit. The self-activating warming pads discussed in Chapter Five will work great here, or use a hot-water bottle. Place the heat source near or around the eggs, but do not allow them to touch. Cover with a towel, and keep an eye on the thermometer. You might need to add more heat pads or water bottles to hold up the temperature.

Another alternative is to warm the eggs with your own body. I'm not suggesting you sit on them, of course, but I've talked to a great many female aviculturists who have admitted to stuffing eggs into their bras in an emergency. I also heard the story of a male aviculturist who was trapped in the fury of Hurricane Andrew several years ago. As the storm ripped his house apart, he grabbed a pipping cockatoo egg from the incubator, shoved it into his shirt pocket, and headed for safety. Hours later, as he huddled under a shelter with the cockatoo egg under his shirt, he felt motion. A brand new, healthy baby cockatoo chick hatched right then and there. I heard that the chick was appropriately named Andrew.

If you try this, remember that human skin oils can clog the egg pores, so wrap the egg loosely in a tissue first. Do not forget to keep the air cell end elevated. If, for some reason, the eggs do get chilled, don't panic. Embryos past the second week of incubation can often withstand a surprising degree of chilling. My old incubator once conked out when I wasn't home. I returned to find my three-week-old Goffin's eggs cooled down to 72°F (22.2°C). I placed them into a brooder, which promptly overheated them to 102°F (38.9°C) and dehydrated them terribly. Because I work at a bird supply company that sells incubators, I was lucky enough to be able to race to work and grab a replacement unit, even though it was now well past midnight. Obviously, most people wouldn't have that option. I finally got the eggs into the new incubator and stabilized the temperature and humidity. However, I saw no sign of movement in the shells and was convinced they were dead. Because I could still see viable blood vessels, I decided to wait. Three days later, the first chick hatched, followed by his sibling 48 hours later. Both chicks were fine, although the older chick was still slightly dehydrated and required hatch assistance because he was glued to the membrane. You can learn two valuable lessons from this experience.

• First, never give up on an egg until it is absolutely beyond question. If you see any sign of blood supply, it is probably still alive.

• Second, always have a backup. Redundancy is a popular concept in humans and nature, for good reason. Most airplanes have two or more engines so that they will not automatically fall out of the sky if one quits. If you are serious about

Relative Humidity Table

Dry-Bulb Temperature	The Degree Difference Between Dry and Wet Thermometers °F																	
	1	2	3	4	5	6	7	8	9	10	11	12	13	14	15	16	17	18
55°F	94	88	82	76	70	65	59	54	49	43	38	33	28	23	19	14	9	5
60°F	94	89	83	78	73	68	53	58	53	48	43	39	34	30	26	21	17	13
65°F	95	90	85	80	75	70	66	61	56	52	48	44	39	35	31	24	27	20
70°F	95	90	86	81	77	72	68	64	59	55	51	48	44	50	36	33	27	25
75°F	96	91	86	82	78	74	70	66	62	58	54	51	47	44	40	37	34	30
80°F	96	91	87	83	79	75	72	68	64	61	57	54	50	47	44	41	38	35
85°F	96	92	88	84	80	77	73	70	66	63	60	56	53	50	47	44	41	38
90°F	96	92	89	85	81	78	74	71	68	65	61	58	55	52	49	47	44	41
95°F	96	93	89	86	82	79	76	72	69	66	63	60	58	55	52	49	47	44
100°F	96	93	89	86	83	80	77	73	70	68	65	62	59	56	54	51	49	46
105°F	97	93	90	87	84	81	78	75	72	69	66	64	61	58	56	53	51	49

To calculate the relative humidity in an incubator or brooder, subtract the wet-bulb reading from the dry-bulb temperature. For example, if the dry-bulb temperature reads 100°F and the wet-bulb thermometer reads 83°F, the difference between the two is 17°F. Locate the 17 across the top of the chart, and read down the left side to find the dry-bulb temperature of 100°F. The point where the row and the column intersect is the relative humidity percent. According to this example, the relative humidity would be 49 percent.

aviculture, you should aim for backup systems on critical equipment. Buying two of everything is expensive. However, if you save just one clutch, then you have probably recouped your money.

The process of incubating and hatching chicks can be a harrowing one. However, when you are successful, the rewards are great. If things go wrong and you're not successful, take comfort in the fact that you're learning. Next breeding season will find you a little wiser and a lot better able to handle the challenges of breeding parrots.

Average Incubation Periods and Clutch Sizes in Selected Parrot Species

	Species	Incubation Range in Days	Incubation Average	Pip to Hatch Range in Days	Pip to Hatch Average	Clutch Size
Macaws	Blue and gold	23–29	26	1–2	1	2–4
	Green-winged	25–29	26	1–3	1	2–4
	Scarlet	24–29	26	1–3	2	2–4
	Yellow collar	24–27	26	1–3	2	3–4
Cockatoos	Citron	25–29	26	1–3	2	2–3
	Goffin's	23–27	26	1–2	1	2–3
	Moluccan	27–31	28	1–3	2	1–2
	Umbrella	25–30	28	1–3	2	1–2
Africans	Congo grey	27–32	28	1–3	2	3–4
	Senegal parrot	24–32	26	1–2	2	3–4
	Timneh grey	26–32	27	1–2	2	3–4
Amazons	Blue-fronted	24–30	28	1–3	2	3–4
	Double yellow-headed	26–30	28	1–3	2	2–4
	Mexican red-headed	24–29	26	1–3	2	2–4
	Spectacled	23–29	25	1–3	2	3–4
Conures	Green-cheeked	22–25	24	1–2	1	4–6
	Jenday	23–27	26	1–2	1	3–6
	Mitred	23–29	24	1–2	1	3–4
	Sun	23–27	25	1–2	1	3–4
Lories	Blue-streaked	24–28	26	1–2	1	2
	Red lory	23–28	26	1–2	1	2
Other Species	Alexandrines	24–26	25	1–2	1	2–4
	Cockatiels	18–22	20	1–2	1	5–8
	Eclectus	25–30	28	1–3	2	2–3
	Lovebirds	22–25	23	1–2	1	4–6
	Parrotlets	18–22	19	1–2	1	5–7
	Pionus	24–28	26	1–2	1	3–4
	Quaker	22–24	23	1–2	1	5–7

This chart represents incubation periods under optimal conditions. Many factors can affect the process, so actual incubation and hatch times may vary.

Chapter Ten

Neonatal Emergencies: Murphy's Law in Action

A newly hatched parrot chick is an amazing sight—blind, usually naked or sporting only sparse, scraggly down, and completely helpless. These fragile little creatures have a long uphill battle to survive into adulthood. Keeping them alive sometimes seems to be a combination of art and alchemy. Yet, in other ways, they're surprisingly strong and resilient. When something does go wrong, you, the aviculturist, have to recognize and correct the situation. The next chapter discusses raising healthy chicks. This one looks at some of the common problems you might encounter and gives a few suggestions about how to solve these problems.

Lack of Feeding Response

When a healthy chick is ready to eat, it will respond to any pressure on the sides of its beak by vocalizing and making a rapid pumping movement. A chick that does not solicit feeding in this manner might be ill, or it simply might not be hungry. The feeding response is triggered by the body's need for nutrients. A chick that is fed a very watery formula can appear to be full, yet it will continue to beg because it is not able to draw enough nutrition from the thin formula. On the other hand, a chick that is fed a very nutrient-rich formula might not beg even with an empty crop because its nutritional needs have been met for the time being.

Species differences also occur in feeding responses. When I first started breeding birds, I began with cockatiels. As any cockatiel breeder knows, these chicks go nuts at the first sign of food and will climb over each other, scream, and lunge for the syringe. You have to pump the food into them fast and furiously. Next I started breeding small African parrots. When I pulled my first clutch of Senegals to hand-feed, I was convinced they were sick. The chicks ate poorly and regurgitated frequently. I took them to the veterinarian, who ran every test possible. Everything showed that they were perfectly healthy. Shortly thereafter, I was talking with an old-time breeder of

Baby cockatiels have a well-developed feeding response.

African parrots who promptly diagnosed the problem. I was simply trying to feed them too fast. Senegals like to take their time, roll the food around in their mouths, and stare off into space between syringes. When I unwittingly forced them to swallow too rapidly, they responded by regurgitating it back up. I slowed the pace, and the chicks were fine. Keep in mind that weaning chicks will also begin to resist feedings and might even turn their heads and struggle.

Species differences and weaning behaviors aside, if a young chick that should be hungry shows a marked lack of feeding response or refuses food, it indicates a problem. Sometimes, chicks that are cold or dehydrated will refuse food. Begin by increasing the brooder temperature and humidity, and try the feeding again in an hour or so. If the chick will still not eat, call your veterinarian. It is probably ill and requires systemic treatment and fluids. Do not waste any time, because chicks deteriorate rapidly. You will have the best chance of saving the chick if you react promptly.

Slow Crop

Slow crop refers to a delayed passage of food from the crop into the digestive tract. This is often the first sign of systemic illness in young chicks, so you should take it very seriously. However, chilling the chick or feeding cold food can also cause it. Do not attempt to feed the baby until the crop contents have cleared. Adding more food might only exacerbate the problem. If you want, you can give the chick a tiny bit of warm water with digestive enzymes (Prozyme, for example) added. If you do not have Prozyme, you can substitute a tiny pinch of sodium-free meat tenderizer. However, you should never use a version that contains salt. Massage the crop gently to break up any impactions, but be very careful not to force fluids into the windpipe and aspirate the chick. Place the chick back into the brooder, and increase the heat and humidity by a few degrees. If the crop has not emptied in an hour, call your veterinarian.

Crop stasis, which is the complete blockage of food between the crop and the digestive tract, is an extremely grave situation that requires immediate veterinary care. These problems are rarely caused by an actual physical blockage of the crop. However, sometimes it can happen, especially in a chick that might have ingested bedding material. More commonly, the problem is a general shutdown of the digestive system due to overwhelming infection or disease. With intensive medical care, saving a chick that is suffering from bacterial or fungal assault is sometimes possible. However, much depends on how quickly you get it to the veterinarian. The crop will most likely have to be flushed out and the contents removed. Injectible drugs will have to be administered. Plenty of old-time home remedies are out there, including the use of baking soda, Pepto-Bismol, or Maalox. Do not use them! These remedies will do nothing to cure the underlying prob-

lem and are likely to worsen the baby's overall condition. If the crop does not empty completely after warming the chick, adding digestive enzymes, and massaging the crop, then the chick has a more serious problem than simple chilling. Get it to the veterinarian immediately, or it will probably not survive.

Crop Burn

Crop burn occurs when the hand-feeder offers the chick formula that is too hot. The scalding food will burn the tissues in the esophagus and crop, causing injury. In most cases, the damage isn't immediately obvious. The crop will swell and scab over from the inside out. It may eventually rupture and begin to leak food. In severe cases, this injury is fatal. If only a portion of the crop is burned, a veterinarian might be able to remove the damaged tissue surgically and repair the crop. However, the chick will need drugs and supportive care if it is to recover. This is a totally preventable injury and should not be allowed to happen. Always stir the formula thoroughly and test the temperature before feeding. This should be one problem you never have to worry about.

Dehydration

Dehydration is a serious problem that requires immediate attention. A dehydrated chick will appear reddish instead of a healthy pink. Its skin will look pinched and dry. Dehydration often occurs secondary to slow crop but can appear on its own. Mild dehydration might be caused by low humidity in the brooder or by allowing a chick to go too long between feedings. However, it is most often a sign of systemic disease. If the baby's crop is functioning normally, increase the brooder humidity and feed a little Pedialyte to rehydrate the chick. If the condition doesn't improve rapidly, call your veterinarian.

Aspiration

Aspiration occurs when the bird inhales food or fluids into its trachea. This can happen when the breeder attempts to feed a chick that isn't showing a normal feeding response or tries to force food into a reluctant chick. If a large amount of food is inhaled, the baby will probably suffocate and die immediately. If only a small amount is inhaled, the chick might cough, gag, or wheeze. If it is able to cough up the inhaled formula, it might not have further problems. The danger is that some formula may have found its way into the chick's respiratory system, where it will cause irritation and infection. This is known as *aspiration pneumonia*. If a chick appears short of breath or makes any unusual respiratory sounds after hand-feeding, call your veterinarian. A course of antibiotics or antifungals might be required.

Infection and Disease

Dozens of diseases and pathogens can infect parrot chicks. Chapter Seven discusses the most common of these and their usual symptoms. Although some of the symptoms are obvious, some are very subtle. Early detection requires a keen eye and a good sixth sense on the part of the breeder. Even if you can't put your finger on it, you will often know when something is wrong with a chick. At times like this, I think it's important to follow your instincts, and get the chick to the veterinarian. The times when I've lost chicks have been when I've ignored that little voice in my head because I couldn't pin down exactly what was wrong. By the time what is wrong becomes obvious, it is often too late.

In truth, saving a young chick once a disease has taken hold is not always easy. Its immune system is too immature to fight off many of the pathogens that an adult parrot could. With early veterinary intervention, however, some chicks can be saved. At least the disease can be identified before it strikes others in the nursery.

Leg Deformities

Leg deformities are a common problem in baby parrots and can be caused by many different factors. Calcium, phosphorus, and vitamin

D$_3$ deficiencies can cause rickets (soft bones) and splayed legs (lateral deviation of the legs) in growing chicks. Even in chicks with good nutrition, maintaining them on slippery surfaces or with insufficient substrate will often cause their legs to splay. If a chick is suffering from rickets, its legs and wings are extremely susceptible to fractures. It

Hobbling How-to's

To hobble a chick, taping or otherwise pulling the legs into proper alignment is necessary. You can easily do this by taking a small piece of foam rubber and cutting two slits the appropriate distance apart for the chick's legs. Slip this over the chick's legs and up against the body. Make sure that the foam doesn't restrict the chick's cloaca and prevent it from pooping. If you do not have foam rubber handy, you can achieve the same result by taping the legs into alignment with Vetwrap or a similar product. Don't use sticky tape, which will damage the chick's skin and feathers. When you're finished taping, the legs should be parallel to each other. Be careful not to pull them together too close, or you will strain or misalign the joints. Until you are experienced at this procedure, you should let your veterinarian evaluate the problem. Hobbling will not work on older chicks and might cause additional problems.

Splayed leg is a lateral deviation of the leg, usually from the knee joint. It can be caused by many factors, but early correction is often successful.

may break a bone for no apparent reason.

In all cases, early and prompt treatment can sometimes resolve the problem. If an underlying nutritional cause exists, your veterinarian can prescribe the proper supplements to restore nutrients to the body. Broken bones will require splinting or surgical correction. If the bone is allowed to heal improperly, it might need to be rebroken and splinted. In the case of splayed legs, early correction is much more successful. If the cause appears to be poor bedding material, a young chick can be tucked into a paper cup filled with crumpled tissues. This will take most of the weight off the leg and allow it to realign. If the leg does not rapidly improve, hobbling the legs is the next step.

As you have probably noticed, almost every description of illness or injury ends with the advice to call your veterinarian. The truth is, parrot chicks can go downhill very quickly when their health is compromised. Without the right experience, tools, diagnostics, and drugs, you will have very little chance of saving them. A good partnership with your veterinarian will allow you to salvage many chicks that would otherwise not survive.

Beak Deformities

The two most common beak deformities in parrot chicks are scissors beak and mandibular prognathism. Scissors beak, which is most frequently seen in macaws, is a lateral deviation where the upper and lower beak cross each other like scissors. Mandibular prognathism is a fancy term for an underbite, where the upper beak rests inside the lower

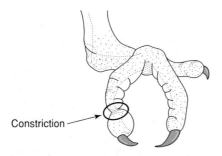

Constriction

Constricted toe syndrome has been linked to low brooder humidity or staphylococcus bacteria.

beak, and is most common in cockatoos. Both of these problems can sometimes be corrected in very young chicks by simply pulling the beak into a normal position and holding it there for a few minutes several times a day. If it does not correct this way, then it will need to be corrected by a veterinarian through the use of a temporary prosthesis. In either case, the treatment is easiest and most successful if performed at an early age while the mandibles are still soft and growing.

Constricted Toe Syndrome

Constricted toe syndrome causes lack of circulation and severe swelling in one or more of a chick's toes. This condition is most common in macaws, African greys, and Eclectus, but it can occur in any species. The affected toe will appear to have something wrapped around it (like a string or thread) that is cutting off the circulation. Actually, a band of tissue has constricted. In mild cases, soaking the toe in warm water and massaging it gently can sometimes restore circulation. DMSO (dimethyl sulfoxide) can reduce swelling and inflammation. If the swelling doesn't go down quickly, your veterinarian will need to cut through the constricted tissue and remove the accumulated fluids. In severe cases, amputating the toe may be necessary.

Chapter Eleven

Rearing Chicks: The Happy Ending

People hand-rear chicks for many reasons. If you're breeding for the pet trade, you'll probably choose to hand-feed and socialize the babies so that they grow into tame, trusting pets. Sometimes the parents refuse to incubate the eggs or feed the hatchlings. In those cases, hand rearing becomes a necessity, not a choice. Whatever your reasons, good nursery management and proper feeding techniques will go a long way toward producing healthy, confident, and well-socialized baby parrots.

The Nursery

If you're operating a large, commercial breeding farm, your nursery is most likely a separate, climate-controlled building with all the latest gadgetry. If you're a small, hobby breeder, your nursery might be a fish tank on your kitchen counter. In either case, how you manage this space will dictate the ultimate health of your chicks. In Chapter Seven disease transmission and quarantine procedures were discussed. The same considerations apply here. The chicks must be situated in a place where they are not exposed to disease from your adult bird aviary. Although housing clutch mates together is fine, keep chicks from different parents in separate brooders. If the parent birds are carrying latent disease, they can transmit the disease to their chicks. The chicks might also receive a level of immunity from the parents so they do not become sick themselves but can pass the illness on to others in the nursery. Even if you pull the eggs for artificial incubation, some diseases infect via *vertical transmission*. This means the hen passes the disease directly into the egg. To be safe, house different clutches separately.

For the same reason, never bring anyone else's chicks into your home or take yours to another location where they might be exposed to other birds. This includes bird fairs, bird club meetings, and even the veterinarian's office. Of course, if a chick is injured or ill, you will need to take it to your veterinarian. From that

To prevent possible disease transmission, chicks from different parents should not be housed together.

point on, though, house it separately. This is called the *closed nursery* concept. It is the only real way to ensure that your babies are safe from disease. It might sound unnecessarily rigid, but parrot neonates (newborn chicks) have poorly developed immune systems. Infections, especially viruses, can spread through a nursery like a wildfire.

Hygiene

Keeping the brooder and nursery area clean is also important. Change the bedding daily or more often as needed. As discussed in Chapter Five, I use paper towels, which can be replaced after every feeding, or cloth diapers and towels, which are easy to replace and launder. I do not recommend pine shavings, corncob, or pelleted grass fiber pellets for use with chicks. They can grow bacteria and fungi quickly and are dangerous if ingested by a youngster. I lost a Senegal chick years ago to ingestion of pine shavings. I've also had several other problems, including chicks with scratched corneas and bacterial infections. Once I stopped using it, all these problems disappeared. A few beddings on the market are made from recycled paper products and are designed to be absorbent and safe if ingested. I've never tried them but I've heard good reports. No matter which bedding you choose, make sure that it is not prone to excessive bacterial and fungal growth, is not ingestible or is safe if ingested, and provides good footing for the babies. Lately, I've heard that some people have been using food items such as oatmeal for substrate. They probably think that it is safe to eat, but they are very wrong. Oatmeal and other foods of that type contain carbohydrates (natural sugars) that provide a perfect growth medium for pathogens. Besides, do you really want your chicks eating food that has been caked with droppings?

Disinfectants

In addition to frequent bedding changes, regularly cleaning and disinfecting the brooder and its surrounding area is important. A vast array of disinfectants is on the market, and choosing one can get pretty confusing. What you really need to understand, however, is that most disinfectants are not cleaners and vice versa. Yes, some products call themselves multipurpose disinfectants and cleaners, but few products on the market can safely and effectively do both. True disinfection is a four-step process: you must first thoroughly clean the item, then rinse it, then apply disinfectant, then rinse again. Disinfectants also have what is known as a contact time. This is the minimum amount of time that the item must spend in contact with the chemical for it to do its job. In most cases, the minimum is 10 minutes. You also must keep in mind that the object needs to remain wet with disinfectant during this whole period. If you wipe on a disinfectant and let it dry immediately, it will be ineffective.

Disinfectants are usually classed in three ways:
• High-level ones are capable of killing all microorganisms.
• Intermediate-level ones will kill almost all bacteria and fungi and also some viruses.
• Low-level ones kill most bacteria and fungi and also some viruses.

The following is a brief rundown of some of the most common types.

Chlorhexidine (Nolvasan) is a good, all-purpose, low-level disinfectant with low toxicity. It can be used as a skin antiseptic and is sometimes given orally (in the drinking water) for the short term to slow the spread of certain viruses and fungi. Dosage is 20 cc per gallon (per 3.8 L) of drinking water for adult birds or 5 cc per gallon (per 3.8 L) of hand-feeding formula for chicks. Do not use orally except under the recommendation of your veterinarian. Nolvasan is not effective against most gram-positive bacteria, *Pseudomonas* bacteria, and nonenveloped viruses, such as polyomavirus. Contact time is 10 minutes, but it loses effectiveness in the presence of organic material.

Quaternary ammonium (Roccal) is a low-level disinfectant that is effective against both gram-negative and gram-positive bacteria and against *Chlamydia*. It is neutralized by contact with soap or organic materials and is not effective against fungi, *Pseudomonas, Mycobacterium,* and nonenveloped viruses. [con]tact time is 10 minutes.

Phenols (1-Stroke Environ, Lysol) are intermediate-level disinfectants effective against most bacteria and some viruses. However, they are not effective against nonenveloped viruses. They are irritating to skin and mucous membranes, so wear gloves and use only with proper ventilation. Contact time is 10 minutes.

Tamed iodines (Vanodine V18, Betadine) are low-level disinfectants and skin antiseptics. They are unstable in the presence of organic material and not effective against *Pseudomonas* or most nonenveloped viruses. Vanodine can be used in the drinking water at a dosage of 5 cc per gallon (per 3.8 L) of water. Contact time is 10 minutes. Intermediate-level disinfection occurs after 30 minutes of contact.

Gluteraldehyde (Wavicide), when used full strength, is a sterilant

There are many different brands of disinfectants on the market.

with a contact time of 10 hours, a high-level disinfectant with a contact time of 45 minutes, and a low-level disinfectant with a contact time of 5 minutes. It is effective against all pathogens, depending on contact time. It is irritating to the skin through direct contact. The fumes are irritating to eyes and mucous membranes. Use only with proper ventilation. This is my disinfectant of choice for soaking feeding syringes and other items where high-level disinfection is important.

Stabilized chlorine dioxide (Dent-A-Gene, Oxyfresh Cleansing Gelé) is an intermediate-level disinfectant effective against most bacteria, fungi, and some viruses. It is effective against some nonenveloped viruses, including polyomavirus. Cleansing Gelé has good detergent action and is one of the few products that functions as a cleaner with disinfectant properties. It is safe and effective for general-purpose use in the aviary. Contact time is 10 minutes.

You will probably find that you use different disinfectants for different applications in your nursery and aviary. In the absence of known disease, you might find that low-level disinfectants are fine for everyday use and resort to the high-level chemicals only for periodic heavy-duty cleaning or in cases of disease outbreak. If you have a diagnosis of disease, check with your veterinarian to determine the most effective disinfectant for that specific pathogen.

Temperature and Humidity

The temperature and humidity at which chicks are maintained is critical to their health. They are not able to regulate their body temperature very well until they are almost completely feathered. In general, keep new hatchlings at about 95°F (35°C) for the first day or so and then reduce the temperature by 1°F (0.5°C) per day down to 90°F (32°C). As the chick's feathers begin to emerge, slowly drop it down to 82°F to 85°F (28°C to 29°C). By the time they are almost completely feathered, drop it down to 72°F to 78°F (22°C to 26°C).

Boosting Humidity

To increase the humidity level in a brooder, cut a piece of sponge to fit inside a shallow crock and add sterile water or a solution of Nolvasan and water. Never put an open dish of water inside a brooder because a tiny chick can climb or fall into it and drown. The sponge will prevent any such mishaps. You can also use a tall jar. However, moisture (humidity) is drawn into the air from the surface of the water, so a shallow but wide crock will offer more surface area (thus higher humidity) than a tall, narrow jar. If you do use a tall jar, drape a clean cloth over the side, and place one end into the jar. The cloth will act as a wick and help disperse moisture into the air.

Chicks that are hungry or uncomfortable will often complain loudly.

Once they are ready for the weaning cage, they can be kept at normal room temperature.

Different species like or will tolerate noticeable differences in the amount of heat. So watch the chicks to see if they are comfortable. For example, in my experience, African parrots and macaws like warmer temperatures, but cockatoos and caique babies prefer less heat. A chick that is too cold will huddle tightly into the bedding, might shiver, and will appear lethargic. A chilled chick might also have slowed crop emptying. A too-warm c___ will fuss and whine, hold its wings away from its body, and might pant or appear flushed. Again, watch the babies and adjust the heat accordingly.

The humidity level that you maintain in the brooder will also affect the chick's welfare. To my knowledge, there haven't been any studies to gauge the effect of various humidity levels on neonatal growth and development. However, a level of 45 to 55 percent relative humidity seems to be the most comfortable. If the humidity is consistently too low, the babies will appear dehydrated and develop dry, flaky skin. If it is too high, it can promote the growth of bacteria and fungi in the brooder.

Feeding the Chicks

Diet is obviously the most essential element to ensure healthy, strong chicks. A variety of good, hand-rearing formulas are on the market, with a wide range of fat and protein levels to choose from. Do not attempt to make your own formula. Plenty of recipes are out there. Each has its supporters who claim that their concoction is superior to any manufactured diet. Although some of these may indeed be fine, the truth is that parrot chicks might survive and grow in spite of a marginal diet, although stunting and permanent developmental deficiencies may occur. For example, some evidence indicates that neonatal African greys fed a substandard diet can grow up to develop behaviors

A stunted chick (left) will usually have a head that is large in proportion to its body. Its legs, toes, wings, and body will appear thin, and it will likely show signs of dehydration, including reddened, dry-looking skin. In contrast, the normal chick (right) is plump, well proportioned, and a healthy pink in color.

Stunted

Normal

similar to attention deficit disorder (ADD) in human children. If you choose a good commercial formula, you will be feeding your babies a product that has been designed and extensively tested to support optimal growth and development.

Nutrient Levels

Which brand you choose is just a matter of personal preference. Most manufacturers offer at least two formulas, with different fat and protein levels. In general, a fat level of 8 to 11 percent and a protein level of 19 to 22 percent is fine for most species except macaws. Amazons, cockatoos, cockatiels, lovebirds, and other species that tend toward obesity should be fed a formula toward the lower end of the range, whereas African parrots and large conures might do best toward the higher end. Macaw chicks must always be fed a formula that is between 12 to 15 percent fat and 19 to 22 percent protein, or stunting can occur. A stunted chick will have a head that is large in proportion to its body, appear thin, and have slowed feather development. In some cases, providing proper nutrition can reverse the condition, but sometimes the damage is permanent.

Once you do choose a formula, resist the urge to doctor it up. Commercially prepared formulas are carefully balanced. The addition of other ingredients might alter the nutritional profile significantly. Many breeders like to add jarred human baby food to the formula, especially vegetable and fruit blends. Adding a small amount of these to the formula of older chicks that are nearing weaning is probably okay. However, I wouldn't recommend it for small chicks. Once again, if you mess up the delicate balance of nutrients, the chicks will suffer.

The same goes for supplements. Vitamins, calcium powders, and other nutritional supplements are not needed and can be dangerous if fed in excess. The only exception I make to this rule is the addition of probiotics and digestive enzymes. These do not alter the nutritional profile and appear to be completely safe.

Probiotics are mixtures of the healthy bacteria that populate the digestive tract of mammals and birds. You are probably familiar with the health benefit of eating yogurt, which is due mostly to its good bacterial content. Most hand-rearing formulas already contain probiotics, but adding a little extra will not hurt the chicks because any excess is excreted. Because these bacteria are fragile, I'm always concerned that those contained in the formula are no longer viable, so I add some fresh right before feeding. It is probably unnecessary, but it is not harmful and makes me feel better.

Digestive enzymes are another supplement that is potentially beneficial. Again, many commercial formulas already contain them, but they are safe to add. These enzymes aid in digestion of the food and presumably make the nutrients more available for assimilation. Although they are not harmful ny way, debate rages over whe er or not they are effective. A study done at the Avicultural Breeding and Research Center in Loxahatchee, Florida, found no improvement in the growth or rate of food passage of Eclectus chicks fed a diet supplemented by digestive enzymes. I have found that these enzymes often work wonders in chicks with mild crop slowdowns caused by environmental factors (such as chilling or minor dehydration). However, I can't swear they have any added benefit for normal, healthy chicks. At any rate, they appear to be perfectly safe, so add them if you wish.

Mixing and Feeding the Formula

One of the most important factors in hand-feeding is the consistency and frequency of the feedings. A good formula is of little use to the chick if it is fed in insufficient quantities. I've seen otherwise good breeders offer their hungry chicks a thin gruel that is barely enough to sustain the babies. The most accurate method of mixing formula is by weight or volume. To mix by volume, add two parts water to one part dry formula, which should produce a mixture that is approximately 27 percent solids. For chicks under two days of age, you can dilute it a little more. For all other ages, the percent solids should fall between 25 to 30 percent to insure proper nutrition. Of course, mixing by volume will vary depending on whether the dry

formula is loose or tightly packed in the measuring cup. A more accurate method is to weigh the ingredients. For example, for each 100 grams of formula, you would want to combine 70 to 75 grams of water with 25 to 30 grams of dry formula to achieve a formula that is 25 to 30 percent solids. Once you've measured it a few times, you'll get a feel for the proper consistency. You can then simply start eyeballing it most of the time, although you should weigh it once in a while to keep yourself accurate.

Temperature

The temperature of the formula is also critical. Too hot, and you will burn the chick's crop, resulting in serious injury. Too cold, and the chick will probably refuse to eat. Formula should be fed between 101°F to 106°F (38.3°C to 41.1°C). Mix it thoroughly, and test with an instant-read thermometer. This probably sounds harsh, but there is *no* excuse for burning a baby's crop. Plenty of emergencies cannot be controlled, but this is not one of them. Stir the formula completely, and test the temperature, period. One of the major causes of hot spots is microwaving the formula. Microwaves heat unevenly. They can overheat and destroy the nutrients in one spot while leaving other areas cold. You can use a microwave, but use it to heat the water only. Then mix in the dry formula, and stir well.

How often you feed will depend on the age of the chicks. In general, from hatch to three days of age, feed every three hours around the clock. From day three until about day ten, feed four times during the day, allowing the chicks to sleep six hours at night without feeding. From day ten until their eyes are fully open, continue to feed four times a day, but let them sleep all the way through the night. Once the chicks' eyes are open and feathers start to emerge, cut back to three feedings a day and then down to two as they approach weaning age. Chicks should have an empty or nearly empty crop when you begin to feed them. If most of the food from the last feeding has not cleared yet, then something is wrong. (See Chapter Ten). Do not attempt to add food to their crop, because this will only worsen the problem. If the food does not clear after another hour or so, then call your veterinarian.

Feeding Utensils and Methods

What you use to feed the chicks is a matter of personal preference. The two most common methods are syringe feeding and spoon-feeding. You can spoon-feed by taking a small metal spoon and bending up the sides to form a V shape. Gently place the tip of the spoon into the chick's mouth, and tilt the spoon up slightly. The chick will pump the spoon and swallow the formula as it flows off. Spoon-feeding can be messy and time consuming. Accurately gauging how much the baby eats is difficult. However, it more

Formula Safety

Two points bear repeating:
• Always mix the formula fresh
• *Never* store mixed formula for use at a later time.

Even under refrigeration, pathogens can grow rapidly in a nutrient-rich formula, turning it into a dangerous bacterial soup.

closely resembles natural feeding by the parent birds. It is also safer than syringe feeding because accidentally aspirating a chick is not as easy.

Syringe feeding is probably the most common method used today. Syringes (without needles) are available in a wide variety of sizes, from 1/2 cc up to 100 cc. There are two common syringe tip styles: luer and catheter. Luer-tip syringes have a

A bent spoon makes an easy and safe hand-feeding tool.

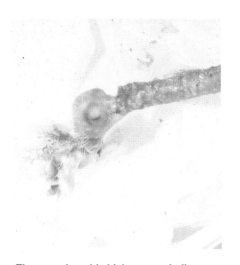

Tiny one-day-old chicks are a challenge to feed.

short, narrow tip and can be used on any size bird. Catheter tips are long and wider. They allow a larger volume of food to pass through quickly, so they make good tools for feeding large birds. In syringe feeding, you hold the syringe in your right hand, place the tip into the left side of the chick's mouth, and gently support its head while you squirt food into its mouth toward the right side. This position is important, because it directs the food toward the chick's esophagus and away from its trachea (windpipe). If too much food goes in at once, the chick can inhale the food (aspirate) and die. Always begin by dribbling the food slowly until the chick begins to pump the syringe. Then depress the plunger to discharge the food at the same rate the chick is swallowing. While the chick is actively pumping, the opening to the trachea closes, so the

chick cannot inhale food. You still must exercise caution, though, so that you do not force food into the chick's mouth while it stops to breathe.

If possible, you should have someone demonstrate hand-feeding a few times before you try it yourself. Older chicks are less likely to aspirate than younger ones. Chicks with a strong feeding response are not as likely to aspirate. The advantages to syringe feeding are that it is quick and easy (after you get the hang of it) and you can tell exactly how much food the chick has eaten.

There is another method of feeding—direct crop feeding. In this method, a length of soft rubber tubing is attached to a syringe. Then the tubing is passed down the chick's throat, directly into its crop. Proponents of this method claim it is faster and safer. I personally dislike the idea of crop feeding, especially when performed by an inexperienced feeder. First of all, I think the chicks must find it unpleasant. People who do this swear the chicks do not mind. How would you feel, though, to have rubber tubing snaked into your stomach every time you wanted a meal? Secondly, I'm concerned that it doesn't allow the babies to properly experience the taste, texture, and warmth of food. I do not know what problems that might cause down the road in terms of healthy eating habits. Finally, it is an invasive procedure. The risks of introducing pathogens, puncturing the esophagus, or tearing the crop all exist. Direct crop feeding is a wonderful method for ill chicks that refuse to feed, but I can't bring myself to recommend it for healthy babies. If you decide to go this route, make sure you use a long enough piece of tubing, because fishing these pieces of rubber out of the crops of chicks who yank them off and swallow them requires veterinary assistance.

No matter which tools you ultimately decide to use, keep them properly disinfected. Do not use the same syringe or spoon on multiple chicks or you risk passing disease around. I usually fill at once all the syringes that I'm going to need, then place them into a bowl of hot water to keep them warm as I feed. As each chick finishes its syringe (or syringes), I toss the used ones into the sink, rinse off my hands, and start with the next chick. Never dip a

Syringe feeding is a common method for feeding chicks. Support the chick's head gently, and place the syringe in the left side of the mouth.

used syringe or spoon back into a dish of formula, as this will also spread disease. If you spoon-feed, make up a separate dish of formula for each chick, or at least for each clutch.

Monitoring Weight

If you are feeding the proper amount of a good formula, a healthy chick should gain weight daily. Weight gain might vary from 10 to 20 percent increase each day and will continue until shortly before weaning. At that time, the chick will start to lose a little weight as it attempts to slim down for flight. You should weigh your chicks every morning before feeding (while their crops are still empty) and record the weights. You will soon have a good feel for what is normal. You will also have valuable records to refer to when the next clutch comes along.

Weigh your chicks every morning before their first feeding.

Removing Chicks from the Nest

If you're allowing the parents to rear the chicks for a while, removing the babies from the nest at the appropriate age is important. Of course, if you want the parents to raise them completely so that you can use them as future breeders, you don't have to worry about this step. If you're raising them for the pet trade and want them to be very tame, you'll probably want to remove them from the nest and complete the rearing process yourself. (As mentioned earlier, some hand-raised babies can still make wonderful breeders, but the focus here is on increasing tameness and handleability.)

I don't like to remove the chicks at a very young age because I want them to know they're parrots and not tiny feathered humans. On the other hand, if you wait too long, they're fearful and hard to feed. Neither extreme presents insurmountable problems. However, a window of time exists that seems perfect for removing chicks from the nest, and that is usually the week after the flight feathers begin to emerge. This can range from two-and-a-half weeks of age in smaller species to about five weeks in macaws. You can pull them earlier, but it doesn't make them any tamer. If you wait much longer, they'll be skittish and require some patience.

All chicks, including incubator-hatched babies fed from day one, go through a short developmental stage in which they become fearful, suspicious, and easily startled. The length and severity of this stage varies by individual. Some birds breeze through it so quickly that you hardly notice. If you happen to pull chicks from the nest at this stage, however, they can be hard to calm for a few days. This stage seems to occur about the time that the first feathers begin to open. After they pass this stage, they usually become calmer and more inquisitive.

Marking Chicks

Marking chicks by banding or microchipping them is a common method of identification. Although microchipping is growing in popularity, most hand-raised chicks are still closed banded. Since these solid leg bands must be placed onto very young chicks, this method of marking is a fairly reliable indication that the bird was born in captivity. The bands are usually coded with information that identifies the breeder, the state in which the breeder resides, and sometimes the year in which the chick was born. Traceable bands are issued by some avicultural organizations, although not all bands are traceable. Chicks are usually banded between about two weeks and four weeks, depending on the species.

To band a chick, begin by obtaining the appropriate band size for that species. The band must be slipped over the chick's foot and onto its ankle while it is still young and the foot is small and somewhat pliable. Begin by gently pulling the longer back toe forward so that you now have three toes pointing forward. Bunch the toes together, and slide the band over the toes and foot. The band should now be resting over the ankle, although the small back toe is probably trapped under the band. Gently work the toe free with your fingers or by sliding a toothpick between the toe and ankle and then carefully pulling the toe free. If you band the chick too early, the band will most likely slip off, so just try again in another day or so. If you wait too long, you will not be able to slide the band over the chick's foot. If it is just a tiny bit tight, a bit of soap will help it slip over. Never try to force on a band that is too small, or you will injure the chick. Using a larger band is not a good idea, either. It will be too loose on the bird and can catch on things and cause injury. If you miss the opportunity to band, you can microchip instead.

Although relatively new to general aviculture, for years many zoos have successfully used microchips to mark and track their animals. This method involves the injection of a small coded microchip (about the size of a grain of rice) into the bird's body (usually the breast muscle). Once implanted, the code can be read by a handheld scanning device, similar to those in use in grocery stores. Once a chip has been placed, it is difficult to remove or tamper with. Microchipping is also

To band a chick, pull the large back toe forward, and slip the band over the three toes and foot, and onto the ankle. The small back toe will probably be trapped under the band.

Gently work the small toe free with your fingers, or slide a toothpick between the toe and ankle, and then carefully pull the toe free. The band should rest comfortably on the ankle when you're finished.

an effective theft deterrent, because reading its code can positively identify a stolen microchipped bird. At present, mostly breeders of large and expensive birds are using microchipping. However, as more and more avian veterinarians begin to offer this service, it may become a method of choice for even the small breeder or pet owner.

Finally, one of the newest options for marking is DNA fingerprinting. In this procedure, a small sample of blood is drawn from the bird and analyzed. Each living creature has its own distinctive DNA, or genetic fingerprint. Identifying an individual by this method is virtually foolproof. This technique is new and relatively expensive but is by far the most reliable method for absolute identification.

Weaning and Socializing Chicks

Without a doubt, weaning is the most stressful time for a baby parrot. It wants to eat on its own, but it is not quite sure how. It wants to lose weight so that it can fly, but it is hungry. During this stage, chicks are often confused and cranky, so it is a stressful time for the breeder as well. Some chicks will beg piteously to be fed and then immediately reject the hand-feeding formula when it is offered. Some chicks become clingy and whiny, and others become aggressive and belligerent. Think of kindergarten children on the first few days of school. Being loving and supportive is important. However, nurturing that growing independence is also important.

Start by offering the chicks a wide variety of colorful and appealing foods. You can begin doing this as soon as you see the chicks beginning to pick at substrate (or poop) in the brooder. Small chunks of fresh fruits and vegetables, breeding pellets, human cereals like Cheerios or Froot Loops, and shelled nuts all make great weaning foods. I do not offer seed to unweaned chicks because I don't want them to get used to having it on a regular basis. Basically, any healthy, nutritious food you can think of can be offered. Avoid foods that have a lot of fat, salt, or sugar, but emphasize taste and texture. During this time, continue to hand-feed two or three times a day. As the babies begin to eat the adult food, cut out the midday feeding. Weighing the chicks daily during this time is important. Although they normally lose a little weight, any significant or sudden weight loss indicates that they're not getting enough to eat.

As they eat greater quantities of adult food, you should gradually eliminate the morning feeding. When they're eating well and maintaining weight, you can cut back on the amount fed at the nighttime feeding and even skip a night if the chicks seem to be doing well. Never forcibly wean a chick, but do not force a disinterested chick to eat, either. Usually, giving up the hand-feeding formula is more of an emotional issue for the chick than an issue of obtaining food. Breeders often create this problem by equating feeding time with love. Think about it: breeders take them from the brooder or weaning cage, make a big fuss, feed them, and then cuddle or play with them. Of course they are going to be reluctant to give up that special time. You can prevent this by making feeding time a short, no-nonsense process and returning the chicks to the weaning cage immediately after they have finished with the formula. Then, a short while later, take them out for cuddles and play time, and offer them a piece of fruit or other treat. Once they make the association that love is separate from the hand-feeding process, they are more emotionally equipped to give up their attachment to the syringe.

My pet Timneh grey, Gizmo, was a late weaner. She would beg incessantly but then refuse the food after one mouthful. I finally realized that she was eating plenty of food on her own, so she was not hungry. However, she was not ready to give up the syringe emotionally—sort of like a kid with a security blanket. After that, when she began to beg, I started putting a little food into a syringe and simply handing it to her. She would play with it for a few minutes and then go eat the adult food. Within a few days, she was completely weaned and the begging stopped.

Proper Socialization

Weaning ease has a lot to do with how well socialized the chicks are. It is, of course, a stage of physical development. However, a confident, secure chick will breeze through the process a lot faster and easier than a fearful, submissive individual. Avoid being overprotective of your chicks. Let them get used to loud noises, sudden movements, and activity. I have a friend who yells "Big noise!" and laughs and claps her hands before she runs the vacuum cleaner. Her chicks, instead of being fearful, respond to her laughter and body language and are soon yelling "Big noise!" themselves whenever loud household noises startle them.

Although properly socialized chicks should show little fear or nervousness around people, they should also learn to respect humans. Parrot chicks, like human children, can become spoiled and obnoxious if they are not raised with loving guidance and discipline. Do not let baby parrots bite, threaten, or playfully attack. Even though these behaviors might be cute in a tiny chick, it will cease to be cute very quickly when the fully grown monster bird flies into a rage and attacks every time it doesn't get its way. A sharp *"No"* coupled with a stern glare is usually enough to stop most chicks in their tracks when they're misbehaving. If that doesn't work, a quick time out in the brooder or weaning cage will give the offender time to contemplate its sins.

Several excellent books are on the market about parrot behavior and psychology. You should read a few to get an idea of the various potential problems and methods of coping. Preventing problem behaviors is much easier than correcting them, so getting your chicks off to a good start will save headaches for both you and the new owners down the line. In general, chicks raised with lots of love, intellectual stimula-

A happy, well-socialized chick is a joy to own. This young Senegal parrot learned to do headstands to amuse itself and its owners.

tion (toys, music, and teaching games, for example), and gentle discipline will grow into healthy and well-adjusted adults. The more exposure a baby parrot has to different people, situations, and noises, the more likely it is to develop the confidence and curiosity it needs. Of course, use common sense. If a chick appears stressed or frightened, then give it a reassuring cuddle and return it to a quieter place until it feels more secure.

I bring my chicks to work with me for hand-feeding. They get used to being picked up and carried around by coworkers. They also have to get used to being bounced around in the portable brooder, riding in the car, and all the strange, loud office noises like ringing telephones and clattering printers. By the time they wean, my chicks are supremely confident and unafraid of strangers. They will immediately run to people and attempt to climb up their leg or into their lap. Most of them also wean early and easily because they're much too busy exploring and making new friends to waste time eating baby food. Of course, all babies are individuals. Some chicks do take longer to wean than others, so be patient. On the other hand, if a chick fails to wean after a reasonable time, continues to beg, and appears thin, it may have an underlying infection. Get it to your veterinarian right away for a checkup.

Average Weights (in Grams) of Selected Parrot Chicks

Age in Days	Senegal Parrot	Goffin's Cockatoo	African Grey (Timneh)	Green-Winged Macaw
Hatch	6–7	8–10	10–14	23–24
1	7–8	9–11	11–15	24–25
2	8–10	11–12	12–15	28–29
3	10–13	13–14	14–18	32–33
4	11–15	14–15	16–20	36–37
5	12–20	16–19	17–22	40–42
6	16–22	20–22	21–29	48–52
7	19–25	24–26	25–35	56–58
8	24–29	27–29	29–39	58–62
9	29–38	32–35	33–47	70–72
10	37–44	36–40	39–58	80–87
11	40–49	45–52	49–64	82–96
12	48–52	46–58	58–67	96–114
13	52–55	52–64	65–70	106–130
14	56–57	62–68	69–73	116–142
15	58–60	69–76	76–84	126–164
16	67–68	76–89	81–93	132–173
17	68–69	82–99	90–111	140–182
18	71–73	95–107	101–121	160–202
19	76–77	98–118	107–130	170–230
20	76–82	108–120	112–133	192–247
21	78–86	121–134	119–139	206–286
4 weeks	102–108	180–196	180–191	360–454
5 weeks	118–132	235–252	221–243	590–630
6 weeks	**141–143**	**240–261**	280–295	864–902
7 weeks	136–139	233–259	301–309	924–1014
8 weeks	125–130	229–250	**326–338**	1092–1153
9 weeks	114–128	224–252	324–330	**1225–1298**
Average adult weight	115–130	225–300	300–350	1000–1200
Average age at weaning	10–12 weeks	14–16 weeks	14–16 weeks	16–20 weeks

Boldfaced ranges are maximum preweaning weight.

Suggested Band Sizes for Select Parrot Species

Species	Suggested Band Sizes	Most Often Used
African grey parrot	14–16	14
Alexandrine parakeet	10–12–14	12
Bare-eyed cockatoo	12–14	14
Blue and gold macaw	16–18–20	18
Blue-crowned conure	10–11–12	10
Blue-fronted Amazon	14–16	14
Bourke's parakeet	Parakeet	Parakeet
Budgerigar	Parakeet	Parakeet
Caiques	10–11–12	10
Chattering lory	10–11–12	Equal
Cherry-headed conure	10–11–12	10
Citron cockatoo	12–14	14
Cockatiel	Cockatiel	Cockatiel
Double yellow-headed Amazon	14–16	Equal
Derbyan parakeet	10–11–12	Equal
Diamond doves	Parakeet	Parakeet
Eclectus parrots	14–16	14
Fig parrots	Cockatiel	Cockatiel
Goffin's cockatoo	12–14	Equal
Gold-capped conure	9	9
Goldies lorikeet	Lovebird	Lovebird
Great-billed parrot	12–14–16	Unsure
Greater sulfur-crested cockatoo	16–18	Equal
Green-cheeked conure	9–cockatiel	Equal
Green-naped lory	9	9
Green-winged macaw	18–20–22	20
Grey-cheeked parakeet	Lovebird–cockatiel	Cockatiel
Hahn's macaw	10–11–12	10
Half-moon conure	9–cockatiel	Equal
Hawk-headed parrot	12–14	12
Hyacinth macaw	20–22–24	20-22
Indian ringneck parakeet	9–9.5 –10	9.5
Jardine's parrot	10–11–12	12
Jenday conure	9–9.5–10	9.5
Kakarikis	Lovebird–cockatiel	Lovebird
Lesser sulfur-crested cockatoo	12–14	Equal
Lilac-crowned Amazon	14–16	14
Lovebird	Lovebird	Lovebird
Maroon-belly conure	9–cockatiel	Cockatiel
Mealy Amazon	14–16	14
Medium sulfur-crested cockatoo	14–16	14
Mexican red-headed Amazon	14–16	14
Meyer's parrot	9–9.5–10	10

Suggested Band Sizes for Select Parrot Species (continued)

Species	Suggested Band Sizes	Most Often Used
Military macaw	16–18–20	18
Mitred conure	10–11–12	12
Moluccan cockatoo	16–18–20	18
Moustache parakeet	9–9.5–10	9
Nanday conure	9–9.5–10	10
Noble macaw	10–11–12	10
Orange-winged Amazon	14–16	14
Panama Amazon	16–18	Equal
Parrotlet	Parakeet–English parakeet–lovebird	English parakeet
Patagonian conure	10–11–12	12
Peach-fronted conure	9	9
Pionus parrots	10–11–12	11
Plum-headed parakeet	Exotic–cockatiel	Cockatiel
Princess of Wales parakeet	9–9.5–10	9–9.5
Quaker (monk) parakeet	Exotic–9–9.5–10	9–9.5
Rainbow lory	9–9.5–10	9.5
Red-bellied parrot	9–9.5–10	10
Red-fronted conure	10	10
Red-fronted macaw	14–16	16
Red-lored Amazon	14	14
Red lory	10–11–12	10
Red-rumped parakeet	Lovebird–cockatiel	Equal
Rock pebbler	9–9.5	Equal
Rose-breasted cockatoo	12–14	12
Rosella	Exotic–9–9.5	Equal
Scarlet macaw	18–20	18
Senegal parrot	9–9.5–10	9.5
Severe macaw	12–14	14
Spectacled Amazon	12–14	12
Sun conure	9–9.5–10	9.5
Timneh grey parrot	12–14	14
Triton cockatoo	16–18	Equal
Turquoisine parakeet	Parakeet	Parakeet
Umbrella cockatoo	14–16–18	16
Violet-necked lory	9	9
White-eyed conure	10	10
Yellow-collared macaw	10–12–14	12
Yellow-crowned Amazon	14	14
Yellow-naped Amazon	14–16	Equal

Chart courtesy of L&M Bird Leg Bands, P.O. Box 2943, San Bernardino, CA 92406
Tel: (909) 882-2649 Fax: (909) 882-5231

Chapter Twelve

Selling Your Babies: The Long Good-bye

Once your chicks are weaned and ready to sell, you will need to consider several issues. Finding a decent, loving home, where your babies can grow and thrive, is of course a major concern. In this lawsuit-crazy world, however, you must also protect yourself from potential legal disputes. To begin, let's discuss where to find a buyer.

Prospective Markets

Several avenues are open for marketing parrot chicks, each with its own good points and bad. If you know first what your ultimate goal is, the process will be a little easier. For example, if you want to insure that your chick goes to an appropriate pet home, your best bet is to sell directly to the potential owner. That way you can work with the owner, answer any questions, and ease the chick's transition into its new family. If you raise large numbers of birds, this can be very time-consuming. You might prefer to sell the babies to a broker or pet shop instead. If

you are breeding parent-raised young, your likely market is other breeders. In any case, be aware of the pitfalls. Control the sale to provide the best possible outcome for everyone involved, especially the chicks.

Individual Pet Homes

By selling directly to the pet owner, you will have a better chance of placing your chicks into a good home and discouraging the impulse purchase that might occur in a pet shop. Don't fool yourself into thinking that you can place a young parrot into an inappropriate home and things will somehow magically work out. They will not. Rescue sanctuaries across the country take in hundreds of abused and unwanted parrots each year, and these are the lucky ones. Many more die or spend their lives stuffed in tiny cages in dark basements because the family becomes bored with the bird or doesn't know how to handle behavioral problems that crop up. I usually tell new owners that I will buy back a chick, or help them find a new home for it, if the relationship doesn't work out. This is admittedly poor business economics, but it helps to ensure that my babies will not wind up as sanctuary birds (or worse) some day.

You certainly cannot ensure that every chick placement is a match made in heaven. However, a few careful discussions with the potential buyers might prevent a lot of headaches on both sides. The disadvantage of selling directly to the pet owner is that much of your time will be spent showing chicks, dispensing advice, and answering questions. It also means inviting strangers into your home, so use appropriate cautions. For example, have a family member or friend present, and get information (name, address, and phone number) about the buyer before you give out your address. I use a post office box and unpublished phone number for my first contact, or have people reach me at work. Once I'm comfortable that they are legitimate, I give my home address and arrange an appointment. A friend of mine was robbed by thieves who answered her ad in the local paper. They knew that exotic birds are pricey and figured she would make a good target. She had no information beyond a (fake) first name, so the police had little to go on.

Pet Shops and Brokers

Pet shops and brokers take much of the risk and work out of selling your chicks. You hand the babies over, and they do the rest. Unfortunately, you also give up the opportunity to screen buyers. Your birds

Parent-reared young might make valuable breeding stock as they mature.

can end up in less-than-desirable homes. Some good shops have personnel that work closely with the customers and aid them in making smart decisions. Brokers usually sell directly to shops or the public. If you go this route, make sure both parties are clear who is responsible for what.

For example, in one case, a local breeder sold $4,000 worth of baby Amazons and macaws to a nearby bird store. The babies were unweaned and unvaccinated, and the pet shop had lovebird chicks in

Factors to Consider Before Selling

Before you sell to a pet home, it is to your advantage and theirs to discuss how the bird will fit into their lives. Obviously, you will not want to sell a large macaw to someone who lives in a studio apartment with cranky neighbors. However, you need to consider plenty of other factors. Some key questions might be the following:

• Do they have small children? Nervous parrots, such as African greys, can find the noise and activity of kids stressful. Macaws do not mind the excitement, but those are awfully big beaks to have around small children. This does not mean they cannot successfully keep one of these species. Make sure, though, that they understand the implications of their choice and the precautions they'll need to take to keep both the kids and the bird safe and happy.

• Do they have other pets? Although dogs, cats, and parrots can and do coexist in peace, a lot depends on the personality of the animals. Cats are natural predators and will view small birds as a potential snack. They usually don't mess with large cockatoos and macaws, but a really large parrot might attack the cat. Dogs are the biggest danger. In just my small circle of friends, I know of five instances of pet dogs attacking and killing parrots. I have a very sweet, gentle dog, but she still isn't allowed to be near an uncaged bird, except under direct and close supervision.

• Where do they live? Again, noisy parrots aren't appropriate for small apartments. Macaws, cockatoos, Amazons, and large conures are probably a bad choice. Most African parrots, Pionus, lovebirds, small conures, and parrotlets are reasonably quiet and can fit into apartment living nicely.

• Do they have the time for a parrot? Some uninitiated folks believe that parrots are akin to aquarium fish and don't require a lot of upkeep and interaction. Clear up these misconceptions quickly and emphatically!

• Do they have the money, space, and dedication to offer proper care? Give them the tools to make the right decisions. Talk about diet, cage requirements, the importance of finding a good veterinarian, and all the other aspects of parrot ownership.

• What do they expect from the bird? If they're just looking for an amusing talking toy, they're bound to be disappointed when they discover the work and love that must be put into forming a relationship with a creature as intelligent as a parrot.

I have a personal policy of not selling a bird to someone whose first question is whether or not I'll guarantee that it will learn to talk. These people are buying a parrot for the wrong reasons. They need to rethink their decision and do a little more research.

stock that were untested carriers of polyomavirus. Within days, the Amazons and macaws contracted polyoma and died. The pet store sued the breeder for selling sick parrots. Of course, the Amazons and macaws were not sick until they were exposed to disease at the store, but it is now a messy legal battle. Imagine a judge trying to understand the intricacies of disease transmission and latent carrier state. On the other hand, who is responsible here? The breeder who sold unvaccinated chicks? The lovebird breeder who sold disease carriers? Or, perhaps, the pet store that put them together without proper quarantine? As you can see, these issues get complicated pretty quickly. You should put together an agreement in writing to be signed by both you and the store or broker.

Bird Fairs

Bird fairs are a good place to meet many interested buyers. Unfortunately, they are also a good place to expose your chicks to disease. As you know from Chapter Seven, many viruses spread easily through the air, on hands, and in several other ways. I do not recommend taking birds to these events. Some smart breeders rent a table and bring a large photo album filled with pictures of the chicks. They can meet people, answer questions, and arrange visits for a later time. Of course, you will lose the short-sighted buyer who wants to make an immediate purchase. However, a savvy pet owner should appreciate the fact that you are operating in the best interests of the chicks.

Other Breeders

Sometimes your best customers can be other breeders who are looking to buy or swap chicks to set up future breeding pairs. They will most likely prefer parent-raised chicks but might work with hand-raised ones. Because they are often looking to pair up a bird they already own, they will need to have proof of the youngster's gender. DNA sexing of chicks is inexpensive, reliable, and easy to perform. In some species, one sex is more rare in captivity than the other, so you might be able to command a

Macaws are not usually a good pet choice for apartment dwellers.

higher price for the less common gender if you sex the chicks.

Pricing and Advertising

If you're not sure what to charge for the species you rear, check out classified ads in your local newspapers to get an idea of selling prices. These are also a good place to advertise your chicks when the time comes. You can look at Internet bird sites for pricing. Be aware, though, that regional price differences exist. In general, parrots are cheaper in the Sunbelt states than in other parts of the country. Local differences will also occur in species pricing. For example, if you're the only person breeding cockatoos in your surrounding area, you'll likely get a little more money than someone breeding an easily available species.

Health Warranties

Health warranties vary widely among breeders. Some folks promise live delivery only—if the bird drops dead in your hands one hour later, you have little recourse. Others have comprehensive warranties that cover the bird for up to a year. Most common is a 72-hour warranty that allows the purchaser to bring the chick to a veterinarian of his or her choice. If the veterinarian finds a problem, the seller has the right to either refund the money or replace the chick. If the buyer doesn't have the bird examined within the 72-hour time frame, then the seller has no further responsibility.

Of course, unless you have this stated in writing, you have little protection. In the case of the pet store polyoma outbreak mentioned earlier, a written warranty of this type might have cleared the breeder of responsibility. In my aviary business, I also require that a comprehensive *necropsy* (animal autopsy) and *histopathology* (a microscopic examination of tissue samples) be performed on any chick of mine that dies during the warranty period. After all, the baby might have died from negligence or exposure to disease after it left my premises. Once you know the cause of death, you and your veterinarian can decide where the responsibility lies and what course of action you need to take.

Sometimes, the responsibility traces back to you quite a while later. I once sold a Senegal parrot to an elderly man who was very lonely since his wife had died. He really loved the bird, and it was his constant companion. About ten months later, I received a call from my veterinarian. The bird had died, and the man's daughter had brought it in for a necropsy. Upon examination, it appeared that the chick suffered from a congenital heart condition (birth defect) that had caused its death. The family didn't know the veterinarian was calling me, and they didn't expect anything from me, because they had owned the bird for nearly a year. I knew in my heart what the ethical answer was, though. I called them up and offered them another Senegal baby. They were thrilled and have since referred numerous people to me. The point is that sometimes a bird will die within a few days, but it is not your fault. Yet other times, a bird will die months later, but you are (or should be) responsible. Get your warranty in writing, and have an experienced avian practitioner diagnose the actual cause of death.

Veterinary exams are important to ensure the health of any new bird. Here a veterinarian swabs the choana (a slit in the hard palate of a bird's mouth) to culture for bacteria.

Health Records and Vaccinations

It's important for both you and the buyer that you maintain careful health records on your flock. If you vaccinate your chicks, keep one copy of the vaccination record in your files and give another copy to the new owners, so that they'll know when the yearly booster shots are due. Record keeping like this is especially important if you sell or trade adult breeder birds. The medical history will help the new owner make intelligent decisions regarding the bird's care. These records can also protect you in the case of a dispute. For example, if a pet shop has a disease outbreak after buying some of your chicks, you'll be in the clear if you can show that your babies were tested for or vaccinated against the disease in question.

Selling Unweaned Chicks

This issue is perhaps one of the most contentious topics in aviculture today. To save time and work, some breeders will sell unweaned chicks at a cheaper price to pet stores or new pet owners. I strongly recommend against it. Hand-feeding requires a great deal of skill and experience. Any mistake can cause the chick's death. Even long-time professional breeders occasionally lose a baby to error, miscalculation, or minor problems that suddenly snowball into major problems. As mentioned earlier, unweaned chicks are also highly susceptible to infection and disease since their immune systems are not yet fully mature.

Do not sell unweaned chicks or you risk a multitude of problems.

One argument frequently heard when someone is trying to justify the sale of young chicks is that hand-feeding by the new owner is necessary so that the chick will bond properly to that person. This is utter nonsense. Parrots are intelligent, sensitive creatures and will bond easily at any age, provided they have been properly socialized as youngsters and are being treated with love and respect. Selling unweaned chicks is never advantageous to the chick. It really benefits only the breeder, who doesn't have to go through the work of weaning. I'm not trying to preach or criticize here—in the past, I sold a few

myself. I've come to believe that it is a mistake, however, and puts the chick at risk. I'm not against selling unweaned chicks to other experienced breeders who have the knowledge to provide proper care, but I do not believe in placing a young chick into the hands of an inexperienced pet owner or into a pet shop with the risk of disease transmission.

Of course, you will have to make these decisions for yourself. Please remember that the safety and welfare of the chicks should always come first. You have put too much love, time, and money into your birds to lose sight of that now.

Troubleshooting Guide

Problem	Possible Causes	See Chapter
Pair doesn't produce eggs	Same sex pair	3, 8
	Pair is not bonded	3
	Poor nutrition	6
	Improper nest box or caging	4
	Old birds	3
Pair produces infertile eggs	Same sex pair (two hens)	3, 8
	Malnutrition	6
	Disease	7
	Improper technique	8
	Improper perching	4, 8
Fertile eggs, dead in shell	Improper incubation	9
	Disease	7
	Malnutrition	6
	Genetic flaw (inbreeding)	1
Late hatch	Low incubation temperature	9
Early hatch, unabsorbed yolk sac	High incubation temperature	9
Poor growth of chick	Wrong hand-feeding formula	11
	Too thin formula	11
	Disease	7
Leg or beak deformities	Calcium deficiency	6, 10, 11
	Improper bedding material	5, 10
Poor feather formation	Malnutrition	6
	Disease (PBFD, polyoma)	7
Slow to wean	Poor nutrition	11
	Emotional reluctance	11
Poor feeding response	Disease	7, 11
	Chick is chilled	11
	Chick is not hungry	11
	Near weaning age	11
	Poor hand-feeding technique	11

Resource Guide

Periodicals

Bird Talk/Birds USA
P.O. Box 6050
Mission Viejo, CA 92690
(949) 855-8822
www.animalnetwork.com

Bird Times
7-L Dundas Circle
Greensboro, NC 27407
(336) 292-4047
www.birdtimes.com

The AFA Watchbird
2208 "A" Artesia Boulevard
Redondo Beach, CA 90278

The Original Flying Machine
10645 N. Tatum Boulevard
Suite 200 #459
Phoenix, AZ 85028
(877) 636-2473
www.originalflyingmachine.com

Organizations

Association of Avian Veterinarians
P.O. Box 811720
Boca Raton, FL 33481
(561) 393-8901
www.aav.org

Midwest Avian Research Expo
   (MARE)
10430 Dewhurst Road
Elyria, OH 44035
(800) 453-5833
www.mare-expo.org

American Federation of Aviculture
P.O. Box 56218
Phoenix, AZ 85079
(602) 484-0931
www.afa.birds.org/

World Parrot Trust
Glanmor House
Hayle, Cornwall TR27 4HY
England
www.worldparrottrust.org

The Gabriel Foundation
P.O. Box 11477
Aspen, CO 81612
(877) 923-1009
www.thegabrielfoundation.org

Mail-order Suppliers

Feeding Tech
1900 S. Anderson Street
Elwood, IN 46036
(765) 552-5812
www.feedingtech.com
(general bird supplies)

Hornbeck's
7088 Lyndon Street
Rosemont, IL 60018
(888) 224-3247 (toll-free)
www.hornbecks.com
(incubators, brooders, disinfectants,
  power failure alarms, general bird
  supplies)

Pet Warehouse
P.O. Box 752138
Dayton, OH 45475
(800) 443-1160
www.petwarehouse.com
(general bird supplies, supplies for
  other animals)

Petiatric Supply
3030 Mascot Street
Wichita, KS 67204
(316) 831-9500
www.petiatric.com
(incubators, brooders)

Manufacturers

AVID Identification Systems, Inc.
3179 Hamner Avenue
Norco, CA 92860
(800) 336-2843
www.avidid.com
(microchipping)

Brinsea Products
3670 S. Hopkins Avenue
Titusville, FL 32780
(407) 267-7009
(incubators, brooders, egg candlers)

Celera AgGen
1756 Picasso Avenue
Davis, CA 95616
(800) 995-2473
(DNA testing and registry)

Dean's Animal Supply, Inc.
P.O. Box 691418
Orlando, FL 32869
(407) 521-2963
(portable brooders)

Humidaire Incubator Co.
217 West Wayne Street
New Madison, OH 45346
(937) 996-3001
(incubators)

Kaytee Products, Inc.
521 Clay Street
Chilton, WI 53014
(800) 669-9580
www.kaytee.com
(Exact bird diets)

Kings Cages LP
145 Sherwood Avenue
Farmingdale, NY 11735
(631) 777-7300
www.kingscage.com
(wrought iron and stainless steel
  cages)

L&M Bird Leg Bands
P.O. Box 2943
San Bernardino, CA 92406
(909) 882-4649
(bird leg bands)

L'Avian Pet Products
Highway 75 S
P.O. Box 359
Stephen, MN 56757
(800) 543-3308
(L'Choice bird diets)

Lafeber Company
24981 N 1400 East Road
Cornell, IL 61319
(800) 842-6445
www.lafeber.com
(bird diets and treats)

Lyon Electric Co.
2765 Main Street
Chula Vista, CA 91911
(619) 585-9900
www.lyonelectric.com
(incubators)

Pretty Bird International, Inc.
5810 Stacy Trail
P.O. Box 177
Stacy, MN 55079
(800) 356-5020
www.prettybird.com
(Pretty Bird bird diets)

Prevue Pet Products, Inc.
224 N. Maplewood Avenue
Chicago, IL 60612
(800) 243-3624
(wrought iron and wire cages)

Rolf C. Hagen U.S.A. Corp
50 Hampden Road
Mansfield, MA 02048
(800) 225-2700
www.pubnix.net/~mhagen
(Tropican bird diets)

Roudybush Inc.
3550 Watt Avenue, Suite 8
Sacramento, CA 95821
(800) 326-1726
www.roudybush.com
(Roudybush bird diets)

Valentine Inc.
4259 S. Western Boulevard
Chicago, IL 60609
(800) 438-7883
(galvanized wire, cage building
    supplies)

Zupreem
P.O. Box 2094
Mission, KS 66202
(800) 345-4767
www.zupreem.com
(Zupreem bird diets)

Bibliography

Alderton, David. *The Atlas of Parrots.* Neptune, NJ: T.F.H. Publications, Inc., 1991.

Avian Medicine: Principles and Application, Branson W. Ritchie, D.V.M., Ph.D., Greg J. Harrison, D.V.M., and Linda R. Harrison (eds.). Lake Worth, FL: Wingers Publishing, Inc., 1997.

Avian Viruses: Function and Control, Branson W. Ritchie, D.V.M., Ph.D., and Linda R. Harrison (eds.). Lake Worth, FL: Wingers Publishing, Inc., 1995.

Burgmann, Petra, D.V.M. *Feeding Your Pet Bird.* Hauppauge, NY: Barron's Educational Series, Inc., 1993.

Coyle, Patrick G. Jr. *Understanding the Life of Birds.* Lakeside, CA: Summit Publications, 1987.

Doane, Bonnie Munro. *The Parrot in Health and Illness: An Owner's Guide.* New York, NY: Howell Book House, 1991.

____. *The Pleasure of Their Company, An Owner's Guide to Parrot Training.* New York, NY: Howell Book House, 1998.

Flammer, Keven, D.V.M., "Measures To Control *Chlamydia psittaci* Infection," in *Proceedings of the Midwest Avian Research Expo,* sponsored by the Midwest Avian Research Expo, 1999.

____. "Management Of The Psittacine Nursery For Improved Health," in *Proceedings of the Midwest Avian Research Expo,* sponsored by the Midwest Avian Research Expo, 1996.

Forshaw, J. M. *Parrots of the World.* Neptune, NJ: T.F.H. Publications, Inc., 1977.

Gallerstein, Gary A., D.V.M. *The Complete Bird Owner's Handbook.* New York, NY: Howell Book House, 1994.

Jordan, Rick. *Parrot Incubation Procedures.* Port Perry, Ontario, Canada: Silvio Mattacchione and Co., 1989.

Juniper, Tony, and Mike Parr. *Parrots: A Guide to Parrots of the World.* New Haven, CT: Yale University Press, 1998.

McDonald, Scott E., D.V.M. "Anatomy And Physiology Of Avian Reproductive Systems," in *Proceedings of the Midwest Avian Research Expo,* sponsored by the Midwest Avian Research Expo, 1996.

____. "Pacheco's Parrot Disease," in *Proceedings of the Midwest Avian Research Expo,* sponsored by the Midwest Avian Research Expo, 1996.

New World Parrots In Crisis: Solutions From Conservation Biology, Steven R. Beissinger and Noel F. R. Snyder (eds.). Washington, DC: Smithsonian Institution Press, 1992.

Perceptions, Conservation & Management of Wild Birds In Trade, Jorgen B. Thomsen, Stephen R. Edwards, and Teresa A. Mulliken (eds.). Cambridge, UK: TRAFFIC International, 1992.

Schubot, Richard M., Kevin J. Clubb, and Susan M. Clubb, D.V.M. *Psittacine Aviculture: Perspectives, Techniques, and Research.* Loxahatchee, FL: Avicultural Breeding and Research Center, 1992.

Spadafori, Gina, and Brian L. Speer, D.V.M. *Birds for Dummies.* Foster City, CA: IDG Books Worldwide, Inc., 1999.

The Wellness Encyclopedia of Food and Nutrition, Sheldon Margen, M.D. (ed.). New York, NY: Health Letter Associates, 1992.

Voren, Howard, and Rick Jordan. *Parrots: Handfeeding and Nursery Management.* Port Perry, Ontario, Canada: Silvio Mattacchione and Co., 1992.

Index